First paperback edition: March 1973
Reprinted July 1977
This new edition: October 1991
Reprinted May 1994

Cover design: Marian Delyth
ISBN: 0 86243 254 5

*The author is donating the royalties of this book
to Cymdeithas yr Iaith Gymraeg.*

Printed and published in Wales
by Y Lolfa Cyf., Talybont, Ceredigion SY24 5HE;
tel (0970) 832 304, fax 832 782.

THE WELSH
EXTREMIST

MODERN WELSH POLITICS, LITERATURE AND SOCIETY

NED THOMAS

y Lolfa

The last chapter in this book is based on a talk given to the 1990 conference of Yr Academi Gymreig, the text of which first appeared in the magazine Planet.

Preface to 1991 Edition

TO REISSUE, twenty years later, a book that was urgent and topical in 1971, is not only to raise one's head recklessly above the parapet, but to become aware oneself of time's many ironies.

The political context inside and outside Wales has changed, almost beyond recognition; attitudes have become harder in many respects, though some wider solidarities have also been built; several important victories have been won for the Welsh language, yet it survives against a darkening background. Even the resonances of some of the words I appeal to—such as 'Socialist'— have changed perceptibly. I would not write the book in exactly the same way now.

For all that, I stand by enough of what I then wrote to want to see a new edition published, all the more so because I know from repeated personal encounters that a new generation has found things in its pages that still touch its life. This in turn reassures me that we shall have transmitted something across the tawdry wasteland of the Thatcher years.

Those who want to know how I look back today on *The Welsh Extremist* and its period should move to the end of this book where I have appended a retrospective essay. Everything that comes before that in the text appears as in the original 1971 Gollancz edition, with the following exceptions: I have corrected one factual error and one mistranslation. I have omitted in its entirety the chapter calling for a Welsh television channel (which has now arrived) because I do not believe that even my most devoted readers should be subjected to the detailed discussion of programme schedules as they were in 1970. Finally I have rewritten a large number of phrases in such a way as to make it absolutely clear to the sensibilites of today that the meaning is inclusive of both women and men, as it was always intended to be.

But I have not updated the statistics, or changed the tenses to take account of the deaths of Kate Roberts or Saunders Lewis since this book was written. In its pages Dafydd Iwan remains forever young, his hand on the strings of his guitar, as in a snapshot of that time of aspirations, against which we can measure to-day's reality.

Preface

THIS BOOK is about the pressures on the Welsh language community, the response to those pressures, and the record of what is happening to us as it can be found in the best modern Welsh literature. It is therefore not chiefly a book about possible constitutional arrangements inside a unitary, federal or dismembered Britain, nor about the economic arguments with which these discussions are often and necessarily bound up. A good deal has already been written on these subjects. Neither am I concerned with party politics in the sense that I assess the electoral chances of *Plaid Cymru*, or state the case for or against the party. Too many imponderables are involved in the crystallization of discontents and aspirations around particular political movements for prediction to be much more than covert propaganda.

But since I constantly touch on politics and economics, I owe the reader in advance a statement of where I stand. As a socialist I believe in the principle of spreading power and wherever possible putting it into the hands of those groups of people who have interests and problems in common. But at the same time I cannot pretend that the urgency of these problems, the political pressure for devolution, is the same everywhere. I think there are pressing reasons throughout Wales why we should be allowed to take, through an elected assembly, the decisions that affect out lives; but I know that pressing as these reasons are for some English-speaking Welsh people, they cannot have the urgency they have for

Welsh-speakers who see their culture in crisis, their separate consciousness threatened with extinction.

The relationship between the two language groups therefore becomes crucial to any political solution. If English-speakers, for economic and other reasons, press for and obtain the power to make decisions here in Wales democratically, they will at the same time produce a situation in which there is hope that the problems of the Welsh speakers can be solved; but if they do not, then those problems still remain, indeed become more aggravated, since the constitutional way out will then seem to be closed.

It is because of these uncertainties that I seem to vacillate between two assumptions: that there is a way out through political and institutional change; and that the Welsh consciousness is condemned (and at the same time privileged) to be a perpetual strain of protest in a society that does not have humane priorities.

Things will work themselves out as they must. This is not a book of answers or predictions, nor is my aim to plead or to warn; it is rather to help people outside, and particularly English people, understand some of the depth of conviction, the secret springs of emotion, the difference and strength of tradition, and the psychology of the Welsh national movement. These are the constant and powerful forces which will be with us, and which will bear on Welsh politics, while the Welsh language and the consciousness of being Welsh exists.

I owe thanks, in different ways, to two Welsh bodies: the Welsh Arts Council, who, by giving me a writer's bursary to complete a novel, helped me to return as a writer to Wales and thus to realize that there was another book that needed writing more urgently; and the Welsh Language Society whose resolution has shamed me, and many other Welsh people, out of our defeatism. Also to Gwyn Williams, Trefenter, who was kind enough to read the typescript.

1 / The Welsh Extremist

I HAD grown up with the word *extremist* almost constantly in my newspaper—Kenya, Cyprus, Israel, Malaya, Aden; very often the word changed to *terrorist* and then one day the words would disappear and the head of a new independent state would arrive in London to meet the Queen. Britain was probably not always wholly wrong, as she was certainly not always right, but most of the time one was too far away to look into the stresses, grievances, philosophies behind the distant violence. *Extremist* put them all beyond the pale, or rather asserted that they had put themselves outside the community of reasonable men.

It was 1968 before I heard the word used about some of my own countrymen, the Welsh. I was living in London at the time, and although the bomb incidents in Wales and the antics of the Free Wales Army in the press and on television were of greater interest to me than to the average English person, these things still passed more or less at the margins of my consciousness. It was some time since I had lived in Wales, the stream of news reporting flows on, no-one can keep up with everything, and 1968 was, after all, the year in which the Russians invaded Czechoslovakia.

As it happens I have a brief record of what I then thought about the Welsh political situation, so far as I thought about it at all. I was editing the British Government's Russian language quarterly circulating in the Soviet Union, and in an article on the Welsh *eis-*

teddfod I noted that as well as considerable cultural differentiation from England there were signs of growing national feeling in the political sphere. The first Welsh Nationalist M.P. had been elected to Parliament, but there were thirty-five other seats in Wales, and until several more of these fell to the Nationalists one could not speak of strong political nationalism. The implication was that since Welshmen had the vote, the future was in their hands.

In 1969 I came to live in Wales, and it did not take me long to realize that this assessment in the conventional terms of British parliamentary democracy was an over-simplification to the point of untruth. I was immediately struck by the translucency of the political situation—the way the bones stood out as in an X-ray from the soft mass of party political and constitutional argument. What I saw was not the ritual sparring of the British political parties, the great induced anger over small differences, but total politics as I had observed it in years of living in Spain and the Soviet Union, politics in which the control of institutions was all-important, politics which made people conceal their allegiance lest they suffer in their jobs, or else use their jobs in a political way.

The general assumptions I make about the importance of the economic and institutional structure, and the relative unimportance for Wales of the present formalized British parliamentary democracy, have a great deal in common with critical Marxism or the English New Left. Yet although they appear as assumptions, they have in fact been forced upon me by what I have observed of political life in Wales.

The real political configuration of Wales seems much clearer to me than does that of England. This may be partly due to my own sense of identification, but it is also there in the situation. The contradictions are more apparent in Wales. The picture of a technologically mature, socially humane society, held up with minor variations by both the Conservative and Labour parties, is more obviously false in a country where the unemployment remains well above average, and where the more or less static population figures conceal the fact that in every generation the young and talented have to leave to find a job, while their places are taken by retired people moving to the coastal resorts, people who may come from any part of Britain and have no identification with the local community. A healthy society can absorb a lot of people from another culture, but a society that is drained of its own best talent begins to resent every incursion—the farms bought by English people, the land bought for the sake of the trout stream by the fishing syndicate from the Midland city, the buyers of holiday cottages who price the local young couples out of the market. It does not help to be told that the whole of Wales is a 'development area' when all these processes continue unabated, and one cannot escape the conclusion that regional policy for Wales has been no more than a very slight brake on the destructive march of late capitalism, breaking human communities not for the sake of some better society based on the cities but so that the wheels of production shall spin faster.

The police and the law courts, too, are more obviously an arm of political power where they are used to prosecute and sentence young people who are campaigning for the natural right to have public signs and documents in the two languages of the country and not merely in English.

Sometimes it seems as if the whole of Wales is consumed in endless protest. The immediate reasons why people oppose bringing an artillery range to the Carmarthenshire coast, the drowning of a mid-Wales valley, the second-class treatment of the Welsh language, the last government's Rural Development Board for Central Wales, are different. Yet at a deeper level they

11

connect, or are felt to connect, which comes to the same thing; and this is what distinguishes the protests in Wales from those in some parts of England to preserve the environment, that they converge on a special kind of consciousness which is a national consciousness. All the threats are threats to the Welsh tradition, the protest is protest in the name of a shared past. But it is also protest in the name of the future, the resolve to establish a more just society—one where people have more control, and are more able to preserve what they love.

If Wales were just a collection of disgruntled upland farmers and unemployed miners selling up and moving east as industry in Britain concentrates itself in the London to Manchester corridor, then our people would be just another group of history's passive victims, their protest the backlash of a minority group slow to adjust. If they could be made to feel British and not Welsh, if they could believe the changes were being forced on them in the name of a better and juster society, they would not need to feel disgruntled. The only problems that would remain would be at the level of redundancy payments and removal expenses.

But Wales in the twentieth century has had a small and dedicated intelligentsia, mainly writers, and they have not kept out of politics: writers rarely keep out of politics when there are really important things to be decided. This is where Wales again differs from some other 'development areas' in Britain. The most serious thinking about Wales, the most passionate feeling for it, has been expressed in Welsh, and through Welsh literature Welsh-speakers have access to minds that have identified with them, with their problems, with the part of the world where they live, so that they are is able to make some sense of what has been happening here.

At school the Welsh people have seen history through British eyes. They have themselves probably not read much at all about their own country's past. Welsh literature interprets to them in their own moral terms, in their own emotional terms, the things that have been happening in Wales. What emerges is a whole pattern of culture and its frustration. More and more in modern Welsh literature we catch the note of desperation that is also the note of heroism, and the assertion of a set of values that has been developed in a history of resistance first to landlordism and capitalism and now to the bureaucratic modern state. The language puts people in touch with the intellectual leadership, and the message they get, and in honesty are bound to get, is that Wales is facing its last chance for survival.

But the attraction of the best literature in Welsh is not merely that it identifies with our life: it holds up the ideal of a civilized and humane society, which is an ideal for people in other places. Because of its small size, the Welsh language community feels in extreme form the mindless destruction that is carried out everywhere in the name of economic logic. The pressures that bear on us all, bear on the Welsh language culture to the point of extinguishing it. It is a small battle for humanity that is being fought in this decaying corner of the late capitalist and bureaucratic world, and that is being fought with a certain verve. The great Welsh writers of this century and the movements which they have influenced are revolutionary, not in any fashionable sense, but in a deep and proper sense of the word, in that they challenge the whole system.

The issue is whether a small community, with its own language and culture and values, its literary and intellectual traditions, its own way of seeing the world, it own way of being human, can go on existing in these islands. A whole collection of attitudes and institutions will have to be changed for this to be possible, for the present pattern is driving this community to extinction. And if

13

Britain cannot guarantee people the right to exist within their own culture, then it cannot expect these people to be overscrupulous towards its own democratic institutions.

When I discuss Welsh nationalism with English people I often find myself caught up in a kind of sixth-form debate about constitutions and boundaries and customs unions. If devolution comes about, these things will be important, but they are not the starting point, they are not the source of the deepest and most passionate feelings. Anyone who thinks *that* will be justifiably perplexed that anyone should want to achieve these ends by violent means. People do not talk of dying for Wales (and there are young Welsh people who use these phrases) because of a vision of a Welsh parliament in Cardiff or for the emblems of prestige that go with official nationhood, but because they see a language and a culture and an identity being wiped off the map of the world, and no longer believe that the forms of British democracy can be used to prevent this.

It is invigorating to find a society where political choices are important enough to cause real friction, but at the same time it is disturbing. The Welsh pattern is one in which militancy certainly, and violence possibly, has a logical place.

The word *extremist* purports to refer not to views held but to methods used, yet in fact extreme methods are not easily separated from extreme situations, extreme pressures. Only the most rigorous pacifist would say 'Hungarian extremists threw petrol bombs at Russian tanks in Budapest', because we recognize that these people were fighting for something we sympathize with, and which they felt could not be defended by other means.

Violence for political ends *everywhere* indicates that some people have reached the point where they see no other way out. A parliamentary democracy is unfortunately not a guarantee in itself that social conflicts will always be resolved peacefully or that justice will automatically be done. When it is negro violence in the United States we see the conflict in terms of historical cause and socio-economic pattern; the same in Northern Ireland. So far in Wales we have been talking as if there were a handful of people practising or advocating violence who constituted a wholly isolated current of thought, and had no general social significance.

The night before the Investiture of the Prince of Wales on 1st July 1969, two young Welshmen blew themselves up, presumably by accident, while laying an explosive charge at Government offices in Abergele. In the English press this was an obscure incident, soon drowned by the spate of heraldic news. But the Welsh language press did not fail to note, nor did sensitive Welsh people, that however unnecessary, however misguided the motives that led to them, these were the first deaths in the name of the Welsh national movement. They moved us nearer general national tragedy. They registered a new bitterness and desperation in the Welsh language community. We could not say that these deaths had nothing to do with us and the state of our country. How many more deaths, or victims maimed like the schoolboy Ian Cox following the Investiture at Caernarfon, do we need before we start to ask whether in Wales too there are not grievances and injustices so deep that they cannot be left to the electoral processes alone?

The use of the word 'extremist', as always, hinders understanding. What we have in Wales, and particularly in the Welsh-speaking community, is a situation of extreme stress plus the extreme frustration of attempts to remedy that situation. People feel the pressures in different degrees. One man is a constitutionalist today, but tomorrow believes in direct action. Some people may move in the direction of thinking that violence against property is a legitimate and effective weapon. A few more blundering police actions like those of the summer of 1969 in mid-Wales, a few more trials so full of anomalies as the Free Wales Army trial, and some kind of shift has taken place in the minds of a few more Welsh people.

The Welsh language community, like every other national community, is a series of overlapping groups, and some of these overlap with the non-Welsh-speaking Welsh. There are members of *Plaid Cymru* who deplore the direct action of the Welsh Language Society, and there are others who approve it. The Welsh Language Society itself deplores violence, yet its members collected money for the families of the two men who died in the Abergele explosion. No group is absolutely stable; people are always moving at the edges of such groups, and everyone can understand, sometimes sympathize with the motives of people whose actions they cannot approve. What I am saying is that in the end the members of a nation are like the members of a family: with all their quarrels and antagonisms they know each other better than anyone outside does, and are held together by a kind of love.

The point was put better than I can put it in a letter to the Welsh weekly *Y Faner* by Dr.Bobi Jones, a poet and a lecturer in Welsh at the University College in Aberystwyth. He was defending having written a poem to the two men killed at Abergele:

> I am a nationalist of the pen, an armchair pacifist. I do not believe that violence is right. When it comes to 'matters of principle' and the like, I come to rest comfortably among the safe, domesticated, respectable majority that believes explosions to be dangerous; and I will cry 'shame' with the rest of the crowd.
>
> No, I don't agree with these lads, and if they were face-to-face with me in the armchair, I should tell them so straight from the shoulder with complete

fearlessness. But they are not here to discuss nice hypotheses about the right way to free Wales. . . Everyone who has in the least assisted in the psychological and material subjection of Wales is responsible for their deaths. Everyone who has been indifferent is responsible. Everyone who supported the great circus at Caernarfon is responsible. And everyone who has ever worked to free Wales from her servility is responsible. . . There is something unseemly in any attempt to be wise in the presence of a fact of this kind that is new in the recent history of Wales. In the midst of our constitutional comforts let us not lose the humanity to see the immeasurable and terrible difference between ourselves and those who risk—and lose—their lives.

This letter, with which I could not disagree, illustrates the moral corruption which is introduced into the situation by violence. It is not merely a question of those who commit acts of violence. There are very many more who in some sense acquiesce. I should find it impossible to hand over to the police a Welsh bomb-layer. I would understand too well the pressures which bore on him. Nor can one pretend that violence sets back the cause of constitutional nationalism. This is a pious lie which it is in the interests both of the British parties and of *Plaid Cymru* to uphold. In fact constitutional and linguistic concessions to Wales have been most numerous in the period of multiplying bomb incidents. And once one acquiesces to the extent of disapproving of violence 'in principle' and not in practice, that principle becomes very hard to distinguish from cowardice.

The most hopeful course for an honest Welsh person, it seems to me, is to back the non-violent civil disobedience campaigns of the Welsh Language Society. They threaten nobody except entrenched authority. They stand for justice of the Welsh-speaker and the English-speaker in Wales. Civil disobedience is not the slippery slope to violence, but an alternative to it, provided enough people join the movement to make it effective.

In the summer of 1969 I was passing through Swansea and looked in on an afternoon session of the lengthy Free Wales Army Trial. The proceedings were just about to recommence and, as the defendants filed into the court, some two-thirds of those in the public gallery rose to their feet and sang the Welsh national anthem. I had some three seconds in which to decide what I should do. Of course I stood up, scrutinized as everyone else there was by some half-dozen policemen on the floor of the court. I have little to say for the methods or intelligence of the FWA. What this incident revealed to me, though in a merely symbolic way, was the meaning of polarization. When conflicts get to a certain pitch you find yourself on the same side as people you do not much approve of.

Ordinary English people have a great natural tolerance. They cannot understand why there should be bombs in Wales, or militant demonstrations. They are very sympathetic to the Welsh language and cannot understand what threatens it. The Welsh-speaker, even when a political nationalist, has hitherto been a natural pacifist. Somewhere in between, a structure of political and economic power has arisen that makes the one feel oppressed by the other, sometimes to the point of taking violent action.

There is a kind of English person, and they can be a certain kind of Tory, though more likely to think of themselves as Socialist, who is concerned not with power and size but with quality of life, who has read Leavis and Lawrence, Forster and Orwell, who realizes that a language is something that people rightly want to preserve, that community is not something to be lamented when you have lost it in new towns and housing estates, but to be cherished where you have it; who is revolutionary enough to believe that things really can be changed, that we can imagine something better than our present society and move towards it, and who is flexible enough to understand that the small breaks for humanity do not always come in the expected places or with the old red banner storming the barricades.

It is for this kind of English person that my book is written. He or she should be in no doubt that their own equivalent in the Welsh-speaking community, indeed that culture itself, is at present held down by a structure of provincial power of the sort they would despise. Until the Welsh language passes out of existence, the best of every generation who speak it will go on fighting in one way or another, not becasue of some narrow obsession, not because they are incapable of feeling themselves part of a wider world-community, but because you cannot set out to contribute to this wider community or take part in the world's moral struggles and accept on your own doorstep a situation which denies your own identity as a Welsh-speaker and the value of the centuries which lie behind you.

2 / English Socialists and Welsh Nationalists

THE WELSH language community does not have defenders in England among those educated, liberal English people who sympathize with minorities everywhere, from the Nagas to the Basques. They are unconcerned about the depth of resentment within the Welsh-speaking community because they are unaware of it.

Everywhere in the world you can travel superficially, see things from the outside, repeat the clichés when you come home; but nowhere is this easier than for the English in Wales. They need never be undeceived in their picture of a pastoral landscape, quaint place-names and a strange language overheard in country towns. There will always be people on hand to speak their own language, in a metaphoric as well as a literal sense, people who might have walked off a golf-course in Surrey, who speak with affectionate patronage of the Welsh language, who may occasionally even speak it and wear it as an adornment but be quick to reassure the foreigner that they do not hold with 'extremism'.

How many English people have ever thought of learning the Welsh language? Very few, because the image of Wales in England (well-represented in Evelyn Waugh) is provincial, unglamorous and comic. Without access to the language and literature, the English are condemned to have that image reinforced by the quaint externals—the trousered *eisteddfod* druids invented in the nineteenth century, not the tradition of Welsh verse going back to the Dark Ages; the singing chapels, not the great mystical poetry of the Welsh nation which has taken the form of hymns.

A special kind of Anglo-Welsh literature grew up, now mercifully on the decline, which lent support to the stereotypes by presenting rich fruity characters speaking a fantastic dialect of English and spilling over with words and emotion. This is the sort of synthetic identity that always arises when a minority nation has to make its way in conditions of cultural dominance. The same *ersatz* emblematic approach to nationhood is found in the Scotland of tartan and haggis. If this is what the other cultures of the British Isles are like, the educated English have every reason to despise them.

Certainly I am not objecting to the Welsh as a music-hall joke; after all, Welsh drama has its stock funny Englishman. But that these should be the only terms in which Welsh culture is understood is a great loss, as if Spain were to be thought of as all castanets and no Lorca.

It is also part of the pattern that the Welsh have been two-faced: the one face turned towards England and concerned with getting on (again like the Scots), accepting the stereotype of the Welshman as a mask until sometimes the face grew to fit it; the other face looking away from England, *having* to look away to survive.

The second face has a defensive, even hostile look. English culture comes mixed up with all the commercialism and triviality of the metropolitan machine. It is easy for Welsh intellectuals to feel that they guard the true function of the artist—to suffer and record—against the smart fashions that pass for art and are backed by the power of large newspapers and publishers with world markets.

The British Council spreads the work of quite minor contemporary English writers round the world. When a

21

Welsh book is translated into English, it no doubt has as much chance of being bought by the British Council as any other book. But a small language needs a different kind of help. It needs translations of its literature to be commissioned. Who is better served, small nations in the Soviet Union such as the Georgians or the Avars, whose writers are translated not only into Russian but also into English and French, but always subject to ideological controls; or the Welsh who have complete freedom to write what they like but not economic power to make their literature known, while their money, like everyone else's in Britain, goes to boost English cultural prestige round the world? As I look at the really good books on my shelves, in Russian and English translation, that have emerged from the small nations of the Soviet Union despite the political censorship, I am not at all sure that we are better off.

Russia offers another and different kind of parallel. The relation between Russian and Georgian writers has been close and fruitful. Because institutions and governments are oppressive there is no reason why individuals should not understand each other. Russians and Georgians have constantly translated each other's work, and each group has been a great support to the other in difficult times, as one sees, very touchingly, in Pasternak's *Letters to Georgian Friends*.

In Welsh literature English people could have found a self-confidence in the role of the writer, the picture of a closer and less class-obstructed relationship with the public, the picture of a relatively untrivialized culture that might have been a support to them in their struggle against the trivialization of their own; and the Welsh should have been able to find better allies than they have done in the nation that has produced in this century Forster and Lawrence and Orwell.

There has been one great difference between the

Russian and British situations. The great Russian writers have been as much victims of their government as the Georgians have. The English liberal intellectuals have managed to go on believing in their democratic institutions. These have served remarkably well in the past to sort out the main conflicts in British society. But no Welsh issue can be a major conflict in Britain because only 2½ million people are involved. When the two large parties steer towards an election, when the 'issues' are discussed in solemn television debates, the choices are usually quite irrelevant to the Welsh voters' real interest. They are persuaded of the importance of a choice that will not radically affect their interests. This is compatible with some degree of real democracy in England.

But in England too the left-wing intellectual has come to realize that the democratic choices are narrow and largely conditioned by the structure of the parties, the mass media, the trade unions and other institutions. Perhaps the Welsh will get more understanding as the educated English realize that many of the things which deny human priorities in Wales are things which frustrate everywhere the creation of a civilized community.

The party system in particular drives a wedge between English and Welsh of fundamentally similar conviction. By today the Labour Party in Wales is the party of the *status quo*, the Unionist party. But at the same time in British terms it likes to think of itself as the party of change. It must therefore insist that its enemies in Wales are reactionary, even 'Fascist', a word I have heard used by more than one Labour M.P. for the nationalists.

But anyone who has met the Welsh nationalist movement knows what a curious blend it is of co-operative socialism and Christianity, internationalism and pacifism; in some ways more traditionalist than the Labour Party (more attached to small units for local government) it is in other spheres (co-operative ownership or foreign policy) much further left. One of the most difficult things, and at the same time the most important things for *Plaid Cymru*, is to get its case across to the English socialist over the heads of the entrenched interest of the Labour Party and the unions which are all based on centralized power.

I have in front of me a rousing attack on Welsh and Scottish nationalism written by Paul Johnson in the *New Statesman*. The title, 'Nationalist Cloud Cuckoo-land' suggests the tone, and it is the sort of piece that in a good old-fashioned way reinforces the convictions of those who already think that way without giving anyone else the least reason to change their minds.

I should not think that Paul Johnson took it very seriously or would want to be judged on this performance: it was written in a news-empty summer week of 1968, probably after having lunch with a worried South Wales Labour M.P. But it is precisely because it reinforces commonly heard fears and prejudices, because it is a compendium of the stock emotional reactions to the idea of breaking up the U.K., that it is worth taking seriously.

> The first thing that strikes me is the essentially negative quality of nationalist propaganda. It has the grumbling, mumbling, small-minded pettiness of the back-row critic, the man who wants to break up the team, the show, the club, the enterprise, the expedition, because all is not going according to plan, and he lacks faith in the future.

Yes, Paul Johnson has something. The Welsh language press does sometimes seem committed to cultivating every minor grievance: a local postmaster is refused permission to put up a Welsh sign on the front of his shop, someone refuses to pay their electricity bill until it comes bilingually and is taken to court. Of course these are trivial grievances. Should we not be thinking about Biafra and Vietnam and Czechoslovaka?

Yet the real pettiness is in the bureaucracy which cannot understand that in a country with two languages all these things stand to reason. One of the most humiliating things for the educated Welsh is the time and energy they have to spend fighting for what should be unquestioned rights. I suppose one can take comfort from a series of petty victories over bureaucracy, even if the struggle rather demeans life. The alternative is the out-and-out struggle, the language of incompatibles. But the petty grievances do not mean that there is not some bigger and more generous national consciousness trying to get out. To understand that, Paul Johnson would have to read some Welsh literature. But up to a point he is right. People subject to petty oppression do nurse petty grievances.

What about the nationalist as the person 'who wants to break up the team, the show, the club', who lacks faith in the future? I am not too worried by the thought of breaking up institutional arrangements as such, and think I can detect the old public school and imperial values lurking behind the English socialist front, a phenomenon George Orwell reported so well. It is no surprise to find Paul Johnson later on declaiming:

> Lloyd George's wizardry was made to mesmerize not a principality but an empire.

But to me the charge of lacking faith in the future is a serious one. I am not one of those people who believes in irreducible national categories, who sees history as the working out of a special purpose associated with a particular racial or linguistic group. It is quite clear to me that individuals and social groups are at certain times offered greater horizons, greater fulfilment, greater social justice by merging with the larger unit (though respect for minority language groups is one of my tests of social justice). Intelligent Uzbeks and oppressed Uzbeks must have welcomed the coming of Soviet power which brought release from the barbarities of the

25

Emirate of Bokhara—though it cannot have been long before they began to have their doubts.

Britain in her world role has offered generations of educated Welsh scope for their talents and a freer atmosphere in some respects than was tolerated by the Non-conformist sects at home in the period of their dominance. In the Labour movement Welsh radicalism, betrayed by the Liberals, saw a way of solving the desperate problems of wages and unemployment inside a framework that was British and an idealism that was international.

But what has happened to Wales? And what has happened to Britain? And what has happened to British socialism? The questions are inextricable. I agree with Priestley when he writes: 'We don't feel we are living in an audaciously creative country but in a stiff and rather disagreeable one'.

What future does Paul Johnson offer us to have faith in? It is, he feels, a time of readjustment: 'Personally I find it an exciting time in which to live, because our arrogance and complacency have received a brutal shaking, and we are now forcing ourselves to discard baseless assumptions hitherto believed to be self-evident truths.'

One of the most frightening things to me in present-day Britain is the readiness with which marginal innovation is claimed as exciting change. The truth is that the system is unable to imagine how things might really be better. The central offices exert pressure downwards more than they express opinion upwards. The permanent secretariat acquires a momentum of its own, bound up with the career structure. The Government committee sits, the pressure groups submit their (predictable) evidence, P.R. firms are employed to put the best case to the public for the existing institutions, and inevitably something emerges which represents a small compromise with change, but nothing like what was expected by the public opinion which led to the committee being set up. You will get more of the feeling of what change really means at a Welsh pop concert than in, say, the report of the Public Schools Commission.

In industrial relations a phrase such as 'workers' control' is thought to be for cranks and revolutionary students. Certainly it will never be mentioned at a higher level so long as working people are represented by a centralized trade union bureaucracy.

The feeling I am expressing is not a specifically Welsh one; the system bears upon us all. People in these islands are still held down in Orwell's phrase 'by a generation of ghosts'. We now have some socialist ghosts as well.

There is no overall theory that calls people in the developed countries to a faith in the future. But there is a widespread aspiration for a more human life, and whenever there is a crack in the grey mechanized normality, this shows through. Of course one can believe that only intolerable material conditions produce any real movement for change among ordinary people, and that therefore in an age of plenty, we must resign ourselves to the system as it is. But I prefer to believe with Silone that

> Reality is more dramatic, more complex and more uncertain. Man is capable of revolt both under conditions of satiety and under conditions of want and oppression. Whoever denies this human faculty denies the dignity of man and equates him with the beasts of burden. Of course, no law, divine or human, can guarantee that man's revolt will end in victory. But this is one of the risks it is his duty and privilege to take.

Of course people have to come together more and more as the complications of society increase. But do they come together on the basis of co-operation or under the duress of the structures, bureaucratic or commercial, to which they have yielded power? This is the issue everywhere, and it is the issue in Wales. People must be given enough power to negotiate with other groups and to set their own priorities.

One cannot know in advance how a partly or fully self-governing Wales would turn out. Some see us as becoming a very left-wing country because of our radical traditions. Certainly there is in Wales no real Conservatism as this is known in England. Paul Johnson sees it quite differently:

> In narrow-based politics it is always the small in spirit, the provincially greedy, the corrupt wheeler-dealers, the clerical bigots, the anti-sex men, the censors and Samuel Smileses who flourish and dominate: the big men seek wider pastures and find them.

One could not ask for a better list of *New Statesman* villains.

But if there has been corruption in Northern Ireland, is it because they had a degree of separation or not enough? Are there not quite different factors at work? If there is bigotry in Eire, was this created by secession? Where are the Danish anti-sex men now, the Finnish clerical bigots, and which of these narrow-based models, if any, would Wales take after? Only the most naïve view of history could see the size of a state as the main determinant of its character. A much more plausible hypothesis would be that it is *provincial* society, where the most intelligent people have often left for the metropolis, that fosters the wheeler-dealer and the censor, the small in spirit. We know all about these things in present-day Wales.

Eventually it comes to this: what is the best break for the future, the best chance of a civilized life for the people who live in this corner of the planet? In Wales we are still, miraculously, able to love the bit of earth on which we live and to feel our continuity with the truly heroic struggles of our forbears more than our differences with them. In some ways it seems easier to know what to do because our ideals have not become tied up with the institutions which represent the class-structure of the last century. Shall we in the end do better than people do in other places? Perhaps not, though it will be a different pattern of success and error. All one can ask of people is to try to put things right in their own time.

Having appealed to our faith in the future, Paul Johnson turns to economic threats:

> If the Scots and the Welsh have cause to envy the wealth of the South-East—and they have—this is a consequence not of political structure but of economic geography. It can be mitigated only by purposeful policies determined and operated by the Union government. Once this union is dissolved, blind economic forces will inexorably widen the gap, with England eagerly accelerating the process by merging its destinies with the European industrial triangle.

It is not a nice thing to see a Socialist licking his lips over the part that will be played by 'blind economic forces' in the impoverishment of Wales, but of course he has a point: parts of Wales will never be accessible to the large markets—that is economic geography. But *where* you build roads, *where* you keep your railways open, what degree of incentive or direction the state gives to bring industry to a particular area, these are questions of political decision.

In Wales the blind economic forces are doing rather well as things stand now. No British government wants to have high unemployment in decaying regions, but in the end Wales has a total population of only 2½ million, and prosperity in the Midlands is bound, if it comes to a choice, to be more important electorally than prosperity in South Wales.

But isn't the moral of all this that we should all work

harder for a prosperous Britain which could provide more help to all the regions? It may *not* be in the best interests of the British economy to subsidize factories in Mid-Wales. Economic logic might indeed point to the concentration of industry and good communications in a corridor from London to Manchester. Wales would make an excellent holiday playground; more reservoirs could be built here; atomic power stations and artillery ranges could flourish in decent isolation from the main concentrations of population.

The trouble is that this is not a future that allows Wales or the Welsh people to go on existing in anything except a picturesque and geographical sense. The picture I have drawn is already too near the present state of affairs, which is why we cannot wait to see whether the latest in a series of half-hearted attempts to arrest depopulation and solve unemployment will succeed. Where the Welsh language is concerned it does not seem likely that anything other than a Welsh government will find the impetus to initiate a programme that gives it real equality with English.

The talented young Welsh have a choice of futures, and both are bright. One is bright with the tawdry impersonal glitter of late capitalism, the quick succession of fashionable theories of society and the flicker of visual images concealing the permanent and unrelenting pressures, the rotting human societies, and the fundamental worthlessness of much of the work they will be asked to do. If they can identify themselves with this they may make a good career, but if they nurse in their heart, as many Welsh people have done in the past, the idea that they will retire from the commuting and the office life to the traditional, warm, human society that reared them, laden with honours and respected by that society, they will be wrong. They will return to a landscape that has memories and no more. A culture, a language, a society, are not things with existences of their own, to be brought out of hiding for Investitures and folkloric occasions. They are the product of the communal experience and effort of the generations.

The other future is bright with a poetic but possibly tragic light. It is a future in which one identifies with the very human community that still exists in Wales, and decides to resist on our own territory the dehumanizing forces that are to be found everywhere. The home ground is the best place to make a stand, because one needs a greater strength and a greater hope than can now be derived from abstract theory and the authoritarian kind of unity that has ruined the Communist parties of many countries; one needs rich traditions of courage and resourcefulness, the support that literature and turns of speech can give one, and even places. One should not underestimate what it means to live in a country where fields and rivers and hills and villages conserve old and human feelings, and where the consciousness of these things is still widespread and can move one like the contour of a loved face. Here one can hope to live one's resistance out with a spring in the step and with a laugh; here one may manage to bring off a small victory for humanity everywhere; and here, if it had to be, would be the best place to die.

So we salute the Czechs and the Anguilans and the Bretons and the Basques—there are degrees of oppression far worse than we know, and there are far worse enemies than Paul Johnson. It would be strange if we did not have a lot in common with the English after all this time, a lot in common with *New Statesman* readers. Perhaps we *are New Statesman* readers, and if we could get our point across, what true English socialist would be against us?

Why then is Paul Johnson against us? There is the question of power. It is the people in the central institutions, the permanent officers, the party *apparatchiki* that are directly endangered by a split-up of the United Kingdom, the officials in ministries that will never again be so remote in their control. But there is more to Paul Johnson's hostility than this.

The Welsh criticism of Britain, by today, is fundamentally a criticism of British socialism. British Conservatism has long been rejected by the Welsh people. If the Welsh seats disappear from the House of Commons the Labour Party will lose far more than the Conservatives. But the Labour Party is also less able to conciliate nationalism because it knows that what is at stake is moral leadership. What has thrown us back on our own radical tradition is the lack of humanity, of resolve, and of imagination in British socialism.

Finally Paul Johnson conjures up the spectre of resurgent English nationalism and a little England. 'I, as a Briton, would not wish to live in such a state which I fear would be scarcely less narrow than the Celtic entities which hived off from it'. But could it not be just what England needs? As with an individual, a nation has to be able to love itself before it can do very much for others. England seems to me particularly the victim of a kind of bureaucratic cramp which interlocks with its class-divisions to produce the present impasse; I say *particularly* because at present ordinary English people do not have offered to them the kind of alternative—to build a new society—which the nationalists offer the Welsh. The English politicians remain locked in the old postures. For the submerged aspirations of the English to surface, something much more drastic will be needed than a call in the pages of the *New Statesman* for them to readjust themselves to technological change. But that one day they will surface I do not doubt, and when they do, the England of D.H.Lawrence will join hands with that of Elgar and E.M.Forster. The class identities may be British—one can speak of the British workman or the British ruling classes, but in the true culture of their hearts the English are English as the Welsh are Welsh. One does not speak of British literature.

3 / Yr Iaith—The Language

THE ENGLISH are remarkably unselfconscious about their language and content to use it as a tool. Although they can allow intellectually for the Welsh attachment to the native language, it is something the English find hard to understand emotionally. It must seem a romantic cultural obsession, a communal neurosis.

There *is* an obsession; that must be admitted. A healthy language, like a healthy body, does not need to have its temperature taken all the time; but Welsh-speakers are constantly asking how the language is doing, noticing a contraction here, a small victory there, forecasting doom, pledging themselves to do more, self-consciously buying Welsh books and records, starting Welsh schools and nursery classes, campaigning for equal status for the language in public life.

The first thing to be said is that these things would not have to be striven for so self-consciously if they were provided as a matter of course, which they are in many bilingual or multilingual countries. Welsh-speakers have to assert their identity, because this identity will otherwise not be respected. But why should the Welsh want to assert their identity so badly?

Here we come to the nature of language itself. If language is merely something that clothes the thought, then it may be worth preserving as a cultural ornament, but it is not a question of life and death to you. This rather uneducated view keeps cropping up in the polemics that surround linguistic questions in Wales. Thus Mrs.Eirene White, then a Minister of State at the Welsh Office, could say in August 1968, at a meeting in the week of the National Eisteddfod:

> It is the thoughts to be clothed that matter. Language is but the style in which it is dressed. Let us never forget this or get our priorities wrong. Let us stop short this side of idolatry.

This can be set against some passages from Dr.F.R. Leavis's *English Literature in our time and the University*. 'Language . . . does more than provide an analogue for a 'culture' in that full sense which very much concerns us . . . it is very largely the essential life of a culture'. And further on:

> Such a cultural tradition, like the language which is at the heart of it, has been formed and kept living— that is, changing in response to changing conditions (material, economic and so on)—by continuous collaborative renewal. The participants tend to be hardly conscious of the basic values and assumptions they share.

Anyone who has tried the least bit of literary translation will know which is the truer account of language. Languages are very delicate networks of historically accumulated associations, and a thought in Welsh has innumerable and untraceable connections with the thought of past centuries, with the environment, with the scenery even, with one's mother and father, with *their* mothers and fathers, with the moral and emotional terms in which the community has discussed its differences.

A different language does not assert one's total difference from other groups of the human race, but it registers the degree of difference that in fact exists; it is from the recognition of this that all worthwhile efforts at understanding between groups must start.

I cannot begin to lay out all the minute tracks of consciousness registered by the Welsh language, but I can try to show the areas of greatest importance. In the first place, by its existence, the language tells us that we are Welsh. All the feeling of nationality that is supported for the English by the Queen, the Houses of Parliament, the London policemen, the bewigged judges, the customs officers at Dover and a whole range of political, cultural and popular institutions, rests for the Welsh on the language and literature, and on a few cultural phenomena such as the *eisteddfod* which are closely linked with the language. For centuries the Welsh identity has not been political or institutional but linguistic and literary, and in the last two centuries, religious. 'May the old language continue' says our national anthem. What else could it ask us to preserve?

I do not wholly regret this pattern. It has made us what we are. It is better in the end to belong to an oppressed group than an oppressing one. The Welsh identity is dearer to me precisely because it lacks the strain of militarism and imperialism which is there in the British identity. I should make it clear that I am not exonerating Welshmen from having participated in British imperialism. It is merely that when they did so they did so as Britishers, not as Welshmen. The Welsh language was not part of that imperialism, and as Welsh speakers in their own country the Welsh were themselves the victims of a kind of imperialism.

In his influential radio lecture *Tynged yr Iaith* (The Fate of the Language), Saunders Lewis predicts the death of Welsh as a living language, given present trends, towards the beginning of the twenty-first century, which is to say in my children's lifetime if not in my own. This he sees as the logical conclusion of a policy begun with the Act of Union of 1536 which demoted Welsh from the status of an official language in Wales. From then on the Welsh were tried in English in the courts, had to use English in all dealings with public authority. Saunders Lewis quotes Mathew Arnold as saying, as late as 1852:

> It must always be the desire of the government to render its dominions, as far as possible, homogeneous. Sooner or later the differences of language between England and Wales will probably be effaced . . . an event which is socially and politically so desirable.

Given this attitude in one of the most advanced educationists of the time in England, it is not surprising that Welsh should have been banned, even from the playgrounds of Welsh schools. The 'Welsh Not' (which had an exact parallel in Brittany), a piece of wood hung round the neck, was passed around among the children. A child could get rid of it to another child heard speaking the native language, and the child caught with it by the schoolmaster was caned.

Glyn Jones, the Anglo-Welsh writer, who himself comes from a Welsh-speaking family, writes of his time at Merthyr Tydfil Grammar School in the second decade of this century:

> The establishment might have been in the middle of the Broads or up on the Pennines for all the contact it had with the rich life of the community surrounding it. We had no school *eisteddfod*, we heard nothing of the turbulent industrial history of the town itself, nothing of its Welsh literary associations, nothing of its religious history.

Things have improved slowly in education. Welsh was allowed as a subject, but even now in thoroughly Welsh-speaking areas it is not always the medium of instruction. When it comes to University education, apart from the study of Welsh itself, and Welsh history, teaching is almost entirely in English.

Although government attitudes are not now actively hostile to the Welsh language, established administrative practice regards English as the norm throughout Wales despite the passing of the Welsh Language Act. The use of Welsh in public life is still generally treated as an eccentricity, something to be conceded within limits.

But the battle for the Welsh language is fought on two fronts: it is fought against bureaucracy and administrative convenience, but it is also fought against the sense of inferiority which centuries of official and social contempt have given many Welsh-speakers. One still meets Welsh people—usually of the older generation—who think it is in some way better to speak English. We have been both secretly proud of, and publicly apologetic for, our language. English has been the path of advancement, the language of the upper social strata who in Wales were either English, or Welsh who had left their own traditions behind them. Welsh was the language of tenant farmers and smallholders, later of miners, tinplate workers and quarrymen, of the girls going into service, but also of the poets and singers and preachers who identified themselves with and ministered to these groups. Welsh-speakers lived their life under hatches and their language is still for them the language of their fierce self-respect, while English is often the language of their servility.

The language is, of course, the vehicle of the literature. Literature in fact *is* language used at its highest level. Welsh literature is both the expression of this life under hatches and the escape from it. It is rather as if the English working class had acquired a wholly different language from the upper classes and that great writers had been born into their culture and spoken for it. Welsh literature is the literature of the people not in any self-conscious way, but because Welsh writers have had no other audience but the ordinary Welsh community. They have also had a literary tradition that leads back to the days of Welsh independence, when Welsh literature stood among the literatures of medieval Europe as a prince among his equals. The rediscovery of this past is the rediscovery by the Welsh of their place in Europe. It is a small place but not a provincial one.

It is hard for the modern English to understand how central a literature can be for the dignity of a language and of those who speak it, though the English of the Renaissance would have understood it very well. Ordinary spoken Welsh is highly dialectal, and there are endless stories of people from North and South Wales who have had to communicate with each other in English because of the dialect differences. This has sometimes been presented to Welsh people as an inherent defect of the language, whereas it is simply and obviously the product of a situation in which there have been no national, standardizing institutions. If there had been Welsh organs of government, a Welsh broadcasting corporation, things would now be very different. Much the same applies to the deficiencies of Welsh in technical and scientific vocabulary.

Then there is the slovenliness of much spoken Welsh, the use of English borrowings when perfectly good Welsh words exist, the uncertainty in ordinary people's mind about grammatical points, all the things that are inevitable where little education has been given in the language, and when Welsh-speakers are fed on English by the mass-media and given only occasional contact with educated speakers of their own tongue.

All these tendencies are the creation of the social environment and are reversible, provided people believe that they are so. One great function of our literature is to be an earnest of what is possible in Welsh, to show the full range of feeling and thought which is possible for a Welsh-speaker. Welsh literature tells the Welsh that their language is not inferior and that they have a princely inheritance.

In writing about the language one is writing symbolically about Wales: divided, tattered, half-swamped by English, desperately homely, rough as the cattle-market and coal-face, it yet carries in it this tradition of human princeliness that wants to find its way out into the light. To maintain one's own language, to bring up one's children to speak the language, requires a positive act of will in present-day Wales; and to create a better society, to rise out of our provincialism, require the same sort of act of will.

Saunders Lewis is surely right when he says in the same radio lecture:

> The whole economic tendency in Britain to concentrate industry is pushing Welsh like a rag into the corner, ready to be thrown on the rubbish-heap'.

But the situation is only hopeless, he adds, if we agree to despair. The political tradition of centuries is against the continuance of Welsh. The only way to change things is by struggle and sacrifice, by determination. He cites an individual case of civil disobedience; the Beasleys, a mining family from near Llanelli, who in a district where all the councillors were Welsh-speaking asked for a rate-demand in Welsh, were taken to court more than a dozen times, demanded proceedings in Welsh, had the bailiffs carry their furniture away three times and after eight years obtained a bilingual rate demand. This, says Saunders Lewis, shows how one should set about it. It is a revolutionary act to revive the Welsh language in Wales.

From this radio lecture of Saunders Lewis's sprang the Welsh Language Society and its direct action campaigns. What we must now ask is why this new militancy should have arisen, particularly among the young.

The resolve of individual Welsh people is, of course, involved; and the urgency of the situation is apparent.

But if Welsh-speakers now want to assert the right to live fully in their own language, there must be other social forces which bear on this resolve.

In the first place there is a belief that at last it may be possible. Inside and outside Wales attitudes are less authoritarian, more favourable to the emergence and flowering of all kinds of group identities hitherto suppressed—for example, women, and linguistic and racial minorities throughout the world. The Welsh language movement is one more of these aspirations towards self-realization, and hardly anyone would now publicly justify suppressing the aspiration, though the suppression in fact continues through the inertia of the political, economic and bureaucratic structure and through the presence of entrenched interests.

It must be admitted that the aspiration to be yourself, to use your own language and not to have to emigrate to find work, only arises when the immediate problems of finding work at all, and of feeding your family have eased. The Welsh-language problem is a problem of second-generation British socialism. The Labour Party in Wales demands loyalty for what it has done in the past but our quarrel is not with *that*, it is with the failure to develop further.

Then there is the growing realization, as among the young everywhere, of a connection between all the elements of social structure, that you cannot be a cultural nationalist only.

The language is itself an indicator of what is happening to us, and very often when we speak of defending the language we are in fact, through the language, defending other aspects of our life, and ultimately defending our own right to have some control over the future. The state of the language shows us the state both of the total Welsh-speaking community, and of the small, local communities which go to make it up. The language declines quantitatively through depopulation, emigration, the turning of the Welsh-speaking areas into either holiday and retirement areas, or forestry plantations and national parks, while the young are forced to leave to find work in the English cities. The language declines qualitatively through an education system that has used English as the medium for instructing Welsh children, through mass-media which give a token Welsh-language service, a sort of pain-reliever to a dying culture rather than a service that enables people to live and communicate in their native tongue; through the tardiness of ministries and public bodies to give the language equal status in notices and public documents; through the growth of the large economic unit, the concentration of economic power, processes which, left to themselves, make a whole national culture dependent on decisions taken for reasons not relevant to Wales in places far outside it.

But the Welsh language is not merely an indicator of these things, it is an *immediate* indicator; it requires no interpretation, it is a picture that is taken in at one glance. There are different levels of sophistication at which Welsh-speakers may understand what is happening. But they are bound to make *some* formulation. The language and its condition is something they encounter daily. When you walk through a small town you have not been in before, or visit a school, or move to a new house and meet the neighbours, you are registering how Welsh the place is, how far the decline has gone here, *who* is Welsh-speaking.

In the struggle for the Welsh language all the universal truths of modern politics are brought home to us. We are asked to be tolerant—tolerant of the *status quo* which is not tolerant of our language. We are told to proceed by constitutional means, when experience has taught us quite clearly that only civil disobedience succeeds in shifting officialdom one inch. We are told to abjure all violence when authority itself violates the right of the Welsh-speaker to be himself. Young people have also learnt, like the students in Paris in 1968, that quite as important as the aim which a particular campaign may have is the consciousness that is forged in the process of campaigning.

The late J.R.Jones, professor of philosophy at Swansea, and with Saunders Lewis the chief inspiration of the young Welsh Language Society, speaks of the language as one of the two foci of our distinct identity as Welsh people, the other one being the land of Wales. On this bit of land, expressing themselves and creating their future through the Welsh language, a certain people has lived for centuries. The interpenetration of these two things is what constitutes national consciousness.

That is a way of thinking about Wales that helps to explain many present-day phenomena, and not least, it seems to me, the increasing passion put into the struggle for the language. The Welsh secondary schools have not been started in those parts where the language is attached to farms and traditional communites but by people living in the urbanized areas of South and northeast Wales. The land is not theirs in such a direct way as it is for the rural Welsh. Their sense of Welshness relies more heavily on the sense of distinct identity given by the language. And this of course is a hopeful thing, for a language and a culture which attached itself wholly to a rural pattern of life would really be doomed.

At the beginning of this chapter I said that the Welsh language was for many people an obsession. For all the reasons given in this chapter it carries a symbolic charge out of all proportion to that which one expects to find in every language alongside its function as a tool of communication. There is something ultimately mysterious, because unconscious, in this clinging to the language. It is a question of holding on to an identity, and if this identity were able to flower in other ways, say through political control of our own future, the language would probably not continue to carry the high symbolic charge it carries now.

The deepest investigation of our Welsh identity, which is not separable from our human identity, comes in literature, and it is to this that I now turn. Here, if anywhere, is made explicit what it means to be Welsh, and what our values are. The formulation of values that can guide us into the future seems to me every bit as important to a national consciousness as a sense of one's past, and of overriding importance in Wales where the choice is between resigning ourselves to becoming an anonymous uprooted part of the English proletariat, and imagining a wholly new future for ourselves. The Welsh language is a neurosis which if worked out can transform society.

4 / Gwenallt

I MUST have been thirty years old before I heard Gwenallt's name, and only recently have I read all his poetry. At first there is something shameful in an admission of this sort—rather as if an educated English person had not heard of Eliot. But there is this difference, that while such an English person would be eccentric I was fairly typical.

A remarkably high proportion of Welsh men and women go on to some form of higher education, but even among those who are from Welsh-speaking homes, few are educated in their own language and literature. Except for those who make Welsh their special subject of study, it has been merely one of the many school subjects which one leaves behind. And since sixth-formers aiming at a university place are expected to have some general English culture, they probably come to know Eliot and Auden and the contemporary playwrights writing in English.

My own ignorance of Welsh literature was reinforced by spending the greater part of my school life outside Wales. In this respect I was again typical of many Welsh children growing up in professional families who had to find employment outside Wales. My Welsh was largely domestic and colloquial—I would still find it difficult to write an academic essay in Welsh—and by the time I came to Gwenallt I knew not only more about English literature, but more of Russian and Spanish literature than I did of Welsh.

It was not that I knew nothing at all. I had read some rather simple anthology pieces at school; while at Oxford I had battled with the late medieval Dafydd ap Gwilym, and got some enjoyment from him. I had taught myself something about *cynghanedd*, the complex alliterative patterns of the Welsh strict metres. At home there were books from my parents' days at a Welsh university college—the poets of the time. Williams-Parry I liked in particular.

But whenever I spoke to my English friends about Welsh literature, I felt I was making a special plea for something beautiful but arcane and demanding its own standards of judgement. Eventually I came to accept this valuation for myself and the small amount of Welsh literature which I knew rather confirmed me in my view; it seemed to belong to a technically more intricate, but to a morally oversimplified and lyrically overblown world.

Looking back, I can see that this attitude derived from the low level of my knowledge of Welsh. I had hit in my reading on a period that was the equivalent of a mixture of Wordsworth and Masefield and Housman, while I knew virtually nothing of earlier periods, and nothing of the last forty years, which can claim to be one of the most important in Welsh literature. I was wholly out of touch with the Welsh higher culture which was carried on by a rather small group of people who had few means of communicating with the population at large. In the years I spent at school in Wales I can remember nothing crossing my path that came from the pen of Gwenallt or of Saunders Lewis. Whether this was more the fault of the schools, or of my own orientation towards success through the English examination system I cannot be sure, but I think it must have been a fairly common experience in those days.

It is part of a wider pattern: the person with a strong Welsh cultural background in the family can keep it up by conscious effort—going to Welsh meetings of all sorts, to eisteddfodau, buying Welsh books; but the things that press themselves on everyone's attention—television, advertising, the daily press, the whole commercial side of life, are in English. The person who has no strong motivation, or little time to spare to be consciously Welsh, drifts away from the educated culture and from Welsh, except perhaps as a domestic language.

Then again, the gap between modern literature in Welsh and English so often seemed to be the gap between the country and the city. Many Welsh-speakers have been brought up in rural areas, and for them the language and literature is inseparable from this pre-industrial landscape. The child grows up, becomes a teacher, a civil servant, a lawyer, works in the large English cities, but a corner of the feelings is forever kept inviolate from the ugliness and complexity of urban life with its impersonal relations—and *that* corner is Welsh.

But the corollary of this view is that Welsh literature does not cope with the modern world. I am not thinking of the awkwardness of some of the technical vocabulary translated into Welsh, but of a more serious thing: from what I knew of Welsh literature it seemed as if industrialization, which had marked all our lives, had not really been experienced in Welsh.

In these assumptions I was wrong. There were industrial communities still speaking Welsh in Carmarthenshire that I did not know of. I remember my amazement at discovering, on a visit to a small pit in East Carmarthenshire that the language spoken underground was Welsh. But of course it is not the *setting* of a poem or a novel, or its place of origin than matters. One can observe the modern world with equal hope of arriving at the truth from a flat in the metropolis or from an isolated farm. It is a quality of consciousness that counts, and no modern consciousness, on whatever bit of the earth it bases itself, can ignore the phenomena of urbanization and industrialization. Were there Welsh writers who took this world into their consciousness as they wrote about Wales?

Parallel with the Welsh/English, rural/urban dichotomy in my mind was a doubt about the compatibility of socialism and nationalism. I do not mean nationalism in a strictly political sense, but as pride in traditional forms of Welsh life. The religious and puritanical element was a particular obstacle, and if one speaks to Welsh people in the less conservative professions in England—journalists, television people, teachers—it is to this that they always revert.

It is not hard to construct a picture of a hill country with a conservative ethical code, tribal family systems, attachment to its history, contrasting with a modern, urban, swinging social democracy. And this is a view that can be held when one is out of Wales, or within it and not immersed in what is happening. But everywhere changes, the elements remain perhaps, but the balance and configuration change. It is a special danger for exiles that they ignore this.

I mention all this half-knowledge, this hesitation about modern Welsh literature—which after all is modern Welsh thinking—in order to show how Gwenallt's writing broke across them. He experienced in Wales, and through the Welsh language, in the tensions of his own life, the pull between the rural and industrial cultures, between socialism and nationalism, Marxism and Christianity. Stylistically, linguistically, he included the life of the steelworks and the farm, while not forgetting the long poetic tradition in which he worked. He is our national poet of the century not because he celebrates Wales but because he expresses the passions and tensions at work here without leaving anything out. I am more sure of his greatness because his eventual, religious synthesis is not my own.

At Alltwen, Pontardawe, in the Swansea valley, in an area that was largely Welsh-speaking then but is now highly anglicized, Gwenallt grew up with strikes and depressions and suffering:

> As we rode bicycles stolen from the scrap
> And played rugby for Wales with pigs' bladders
> I never thought I should hear how two of my friends
> Spewed out the dirty red of their lungs into a bucket

The whole picture is there, death by accident, 'the industrial leopard that leaps out sudden-sly', the widows cutting sticks and turning to their Bibles, the graves loaded with 'silicotic roses, lilies pale as gas', 'the dark quiet funerals winding between the thunders of the tinplateworks and the steelworks'.

Brought up in Welsh Calvinistic Methodism he reacted first against institutional Christianity in the direction of the kind of Christian anarchism he found in late Tolstoy, but this view hardened, as he looked around him, into complete rejection of Christianity, and, as he read Lenin, into full Marxism:

> Capitalism was something living to us. We saw the poverty, famine and near-famine, the hovel-like houses, mothers growing old before their time, the cruelty of soldiers and policemen during the strikes, doctors putting tuberculosis instead of silicosis on the death certificate to avoid the paying of compensation to relatives, and the bodies coming home after the accidents. Years later, my father's body came home after he had been burnt to death by molten metal, and that unnecessarily. When, in the funeral sermon, the minister said that it was God's will, I cursed his sermon and his God with all the hauliers' swear-words that I knew, and when they sang the hymn at the graveside, I sang in my heart the *Red Flag*.

But Gwenallt's parents came from Carmarthenshire, and on his visits to relatives there he saw a relatively prosperous farming community living the traditional simple, healthy and godly life; the beauty of the countryside was matched by an orderliness in life and death which gave people a secular dignity as well as their dignity before God. Carmarthenshire is celebrated in a whole series of poems written throughout Gwenallt's lifetime.

It is fair to say that he idealized the old rural life, in this being typical of many Welsh people. It is not that he says things that are not true—Wales in the late eighteenth and ninteenth century *was* a remarkable collection of small, politically radical, religiously cultured communities. In his last poem to Carmarthenshire, written on the occasion of Gwynfor Evans's election as M.P. for that constituency, Gwenallt recalled the mixed political and religious history of the county—the Rebecca riots, the mystical hymn-writer, Williams Pantycelyn. There is a great tradition of courage, of culture, of placing human qualities first, that Welsh people can still feel when they look to this period.

What Gwenallt left out was the rural poverty, the damp cottages, the puritanical repression, the deaths from tuberculosis. Anyhow he did not imagine that we could go back to the old life. The important thing which the Welsh countryside offered him, and which it offers us, is the image of a really human society; and for Gwenallt, humans could only have their proper place when they placed nothing above themselves except God.

When socialists and anarchists analyse the structures of oppression they use the language of Marxism, technical-sounding, Germanic, full of *-isms*. But when they have tried to imagine the good life, how often it is the social relationships of the village that are recalled, with the modern conveniences added.

There is a strong rural strain in socialism. One should not forget that the growth of industry, which herded men into the factories and slums, also broke up the traditional values of the country communities, that here too the pressures became more acute. The country is quite as capable of being revolutionary as the city under a certain degree of pressure and with certain leadership. We have the village communes of the Spanish anarchists in the Civil War, the rural-based revolutions of Castro and Mao. When the vision of Utopia is held out at the end of Brecht's *The Caucasian Chalk Circle*, it is a picture of the ideal rural society:

> But you, you who have listened to the story of the Chalk Circle,
>
> Take note what men of old concluded:
> That what there is shall go to those who are good for it
>
> Thus: the children to the motherly, that they prosper,
>
> The carts to the good drivers, that they are well-driven
> And the valley to the waterers, that it bring forth fruit.

One can hardly imagine a complex industrial society organized on these lines. And yet, this is what our minds must be stimulated to do, to reassert human dignity and supremacy over the impersonal structures which we have created and which now dominate us. The image of the personal, caring, rural community survives not to call us back but to give us strength to create new and more humane ways of living together. I sometimes wonder how to interpret that obscure clause in the *Communist Manifesto* which looks forward to the abolition of the distinction between town and country. It is perhaps obscure enough to allow one a modern metaphorical interpretation—the bringing of people together for necessary social organization without turning them into a mass huddled in the shadow of all-powerful institutions —and also a literal one, that for a truly human life we must spread the population more evenly over the habitable land. The Welsh national movement carries deeply within it the idea that the whole of the country must be developed and repopulated. The ugly proletarian villages of the south and the deserted uplands of the centre are the reverse sides of the same phenomenon, the industrial revolution, which bore on the same nation, the Welsh. They are not two peoples, the hill-farmers and the tin-plate workers; their Christianity and their socialism are not in opposition, but facets of one aspiration. It took Gwenallt to express this sense of unity, of triumph over old (but not *very* old) divisions:

> The span of the Cross is much wider
> Than their Puritanism and their Socialism
>
> And there is a place for the fist of Karl Marx in His Church.
>
> Farm and Furnace march together
> The humanity of the pit, the godliness of the country,
>
> Tawe and Tywi, Canaan and Wales, Earth and Heaven.

All Gwenallt's published poems date from after his return to Christianity. The essay in the symposium *Credaf* (1943) from which the earlier prose quotation came, tells how he became a Christian and a nationalist. He came to suspect that there was an element of power-seeking mixed in with socialist idealism. The unions were there to bargain for more pay. They did not strike to establish socialism, or even to increase the old age pension. He noted that there was a division between the skilled and the unskilled worker, and that only a small and able section of the workers took an interest in union politics. A miner who was a good speaker became a checkweighman, a union official, and moving further and further from the coal-face, ended up in Parliament. 'It was the workers' leaders in Parliament who betrayed the workers on strike,' wrote Gwenallt, thinking probably of how the miners stayed out and were ground into the dust after the General Strike of 1926 had been broken by the Government.

During the First World War Gwenallt had spent two years in Wormwood Scrubs and Dartmoor as a conscientious objector. This is the basis of his early and only novel, *Plasau'r Brenin* (The King's Mansions), a striking if schematic piece of work. When he came out he found that M.P.s who had been in prison for the same cause were voting in favour of more warships: 'Jobs extinguished the fire, power turned rebels into conservatives. Marx showed that self-interest lurked behind bourgeois ideals, and he was right, but couldn't self-interest lurk behind Communist ideals?'

> The Utopia has gone from the top of Gellionen,
> Abstract humanity, the classless and frontierless world;
> And the only things that lie on the floor of memory
> Are family and community, man's suffering and sacrifice.

How suddenly illuminating it is for a Welsh person to find that here, in what is outwardly a rotting province of post-imperial England, the tragedy of European socialism has been experienced and formulated in our own idiom. Here Gwenallt seems to join hands with Silone who left the Abruzzi to follow international Communism, and eventually came back from the theories to his original humanitarian impulse and to write about the society he knew.

Wales now becomes for Gwenallt the image of a human society fighting the pressures of a dehumanizing industrial, military and capitalist structure, identified with the British Empire ('I have hated the British Jezebel since I was a lad of 17'). He admitted that many things had been improved by Socialist governments, but for him the framework was still oppressive, and was bound to be so because Socialists, like other people with purely secular ends, put their own power first. For him the truly human society exists always in the light of God.

When he brought the rural past and the Christian past of Wales to bear on the industrial scene, Gwenallt gave it a new and beautiful colouring. When the miners and steelmen escaped from the inhumanity of their work they kept pigs on smallholdings, dug the garden or attended the chapels which still held out the idea of a worker's precious individual worth. Here, too, people were a community, if a community of suffering, and in asserting their humanity they asserted their divinity. The pigeons released from the top ends of the long gardens that climb up the hillsides from the black terraced houses

> Circle the pillars of smoke in the sky
> Colouring the curve of grey
> A mass of beauty amid the fog,
> The shape of the Holy Spirit above the valley.

We now come to something in Gwenallt—and in Wales—that both socialists and Christians can find hopeful. Religion and rebelliousness are compatible. In reverting to Christianity (though his was never a very conventional faith) Gwenallt did not give up the fight for a better secular order. His religion did not take him away from action in the world as Eliot's did, or Auden's. This I think was because the whole culture with which he identified himself was in a state of resistance to authority. American Negro Christianity offers a parallel. Gwenallt does not separate into religious and political periods and very often the two elements are there in the same poem.

Because Welsh non-conformism identified with the Welsh people, the ordinary Welsh people, at a time when they were largely illiterate and were expected to listen to services conducted in English by the Established Church for the landlord class, it had from the start a courageous and radical face, as important though less well known than its puritanical one. The outsider thinks of the Welsh non-conformist tradition as existing in tension with the broader, more tolerant ways of Anglicanism and secularism. But it has its internal tension, and has always had it, between the puritanism which, in Richard Hoggart's phrase at the Lady Chatterley trial, consists in having 'a strong sense of responsibility to your own conscience' and the puritanism which is a question of social observance. The first current has always had a strong feeling for social justice, and it is this which makes religion a less conservative force in Wales than in England. Moreover this protesting current has always seemed more *Welsh*, since churchmen who supported secular authority, e.g. preaching the just war in 1914-1918, inescapably found themselves supporting *English* authority.

Gwenallt, in his rural poems and his industrial poems, in the connections he draws between the two kinds of Welsh community, has the continuity of Welsh history itself. His religion and his rebelliousness fit a Welsh pattern, run together back into the Welsh past. The chief character of his novel thinks back from prison to his home in Carmarthenshire:

> It was important for the prisoner to keep hold of his memories, he had to hold tight to the past, to the land where he first saw the light of day, to the people whose blood was in his veins, whose strength was in his brain, whose determination was in his soul. If he were to lose his memories he would be like a rootless tree at the mercy of every mad wind.

Because he had a firm hold of this past with its qualities of courage and humanity in a period when many Welsh people—English and Welsh-speaking alike—lost touch with them, he is a great giver of strength; and because he includes in his work currents that have at times seemed to be opposed to each other, he is a great giver of unity.

Perhaps he will eventually be thought of as a religious writer, with some of Péguy's worker-Christianity, some of Simone Weil's pacifism, one of the figures who detaches Christianity from its burden of class allegiance and institutionalism and makes it again worthy of respect. He would have agreed with Andrey Sinyavsky who wrote: 'In the end there is nothing but God, who includes all. But the Church has sinned through being too well brought up. Christ's church has become confused with a finishing school for upper-class girls'. One does not have to be a Christian to see that in some fusion of the Communist ideal of social justice with the valuation which religion puts on the individual soul there lies a hope for a more truly civilized society.

Gwenallt died on Christmas Eve 1968. His lines on Pantycelyn suggest themselves as his own epitaph:

> He looked on Wales as a wilderness under the light of God
> And strove to make her part of the kingdom of Christ.

But there is another line of Gwenallt's that sums up his work as a poet of courage and resistance. He was himself 'the traditional, revolutionary wind' and his poems have been quoted at political meetings up and down Wales.

He looks at the places in Carmarthenshire he knew when he was young. The community has been destroyed, the young have left to find work, the farms are covered with forestry plantations. And it has all been not for the building of a better society but for the concentration of power, for the cultural degradation of people for profit, and for the perpetuation of militarism:

> They have planted the saplings for the third war
> On the lands of Esgeir-Ceir and the fields of Tir-bach
> Near Rhydcymerau.

The poem 'Graves' illustrates his combination of traditional form and contemporary protest. There are some famous old Welsh triads which ask where the various Arthurian heroes are buried. He imitates their form to evoke first the lives of his grandfathers buried at Llansawel in rural Carmarthenshire; then the graves of his father and brother and mother, and the graves of two jolly drinkers in Alltwen in the industrial Swansea Valley. If the poem finished here it would be personally touching and evocative in the way Hardy's best poems are. But in the last verse he generalizes, and asks about another grave:

> And the grave beneath the gorse
> Shows where our language was lost
> Our fine civilization forced.

But Gwenallt was not a poet of resignation, and his fighting spirit is better illustrated by a later poem in which he retells the story of a meeting between Henry II of England and an old man from Pencader. The king asks what hope there can be for the Welsh against his large army. It would be easy to wipe this nation off the map of the world. Not all your power, says the old man, could conquer this country were it not for your allies within: treachery and disunity and job-seeking (this line is as contemporary as ever it was). The weaknesses of my country drive me quite out of my mind, says the old man, but only the anger of God on top or our petty angers can destroy the nation:

> And he will raise up a small band of people
> Who will lead us through these critical times;
> It is *they* who will answer at the day of doom
> For this corner of the world.

5 / Saunders Lewis

THERE IS no way of looking at modern Welsh literature or modern Welsh politics that does not give Saunders Lewis (who died in 1985) the central place. He was one of the founders of *Plaid Cymru* in 1925, and its president in the early period. In 1936, with D.J.Williams and the Rev.Lewis Valentine, he burnt down the aircraft sheds of the R.A.F. bombing school at Penyberth in Caernarfonshire, was convicted and imprisoned after trials which are now seen to have been a psychological turning-point in modern Welsh history. He was always a powerful political and polemical journalist, and in his old age still made effective forays into politics. I have already quoted from his radio lecture *Tynged yr Iaith* (The Fate of the Language) and it is through his inspiration of the Welsh Language Society that his influence has chiefly been felt in the politics of recent years. His name also arises whenever violence is discussed as a means of national liberation, and this is a subject that I shall return to.

But at the same time he has dominated the literary scene, first as a literary critic and later as a dramatist, the finest we have had in Wales, and among the greatest that Europe has produced in this century. He is also a good poet outside the plays, and while he has written only two novels, one of these, *Merch Gwern Hywel*, is among the best in Welsh.

It is an historical novel about the coming of Methodism to Wales—a period as formative and destructive as the

Reformation in English history; and it is not a costume piece, a colourful, picturesque canvas like the novels that have often purported to explain Wales to the English, but an historical novel as Thomas Mann or George Lukács would understand it: the bones of social forces clothed in the flesh of real people, and explaining to us movements in our past which have made us what we are.

In his critical study of Williams Pantycelyn we are taught to see a country hymn-writer for what he was— one of the great Christian mystics of Europe, a deep introspective analyst of spiritual health and disease. Indeed, in most of his criticism Saunders Lewis is concerned to give a European perspective on Wales. In conditions of greater national equality it may one day be possible to write the history of English influences on Welsh literature, but in his time Saunders Lewis's emphasis was an essential one, because he followed a rather provincial century (in which Britain as a whole was isolated from the continental movements) and because failure to make this European emphasis involved allowing the Welsh to regard themselves as a provincial culture inside Britain. We are back with the question of separate identity, psychological identity; we are at a level where politics and literature cannot be kept separate.

As Saunders Lewis's fame has grown outside Welsh-speaking Wales, there has been an attempt to separate the artist from his politics. If politics is regarded narrowly, as the advocating of certain courses of action at particular times, then Saunders Lewis's greatest writing, his plays are not political or propagandist, even when he is writing about present-day Wales. He moves at a deeper level.

But if Welsh politics is more concerned with the rediscovery by Welsh people of their identity, their courage, their sense of the fullness of life *as Welsh people*, then it is precisely this deeper level which is most political. When we also remember that Saunders Lewis's politics are not based on a set of theoretical beliefs, but on the culture and quality of life of a whole nation which he sees himself as defending, then we realize that politics is here a much wider term and not to be kept separate from the kind of experience we find in literature. To separate the two things in the case of Saunders Lewis is to try to 'disinfect' him in the way authority always finds convenient —one thinks of the partial reinstatement of Lorca in Spain in Franco's later years. A time may come, of course, when his work ceases to have a political relevance, but until then, in Solzhenitsyn's words 'A great writer is like an alternative government'.

The story of Penyberth is little known outside Wales, but within the country where it is referred to as the 'Fire in Llŷn' it has gained rather than lost importance with time. After they had burnt down the sheds of the newly-established bombing-school on the Llŷn peninsula in West Caernarfonshire, the three men gave themselves up to the police. They admitted the act and asked to be cleared by a jury of their own countrymen on the grounds that they had acted with moral right on their side, though in breach of the law.

The first defence made by Saunders Lewis at the trial was that they had tried every legitimate constitutional way of protesting against the setting up of the bombing-school in Llŷn: petitions had been drawn up, religious and secular organizations had protested up and down Wales. The Prime Minister refused to meet a delegation to discuss the objections.

Other sites had been turned down for the bombing-school after protests in England. Abbotsbury in Dorset was spared because of its breeding swans. Holy Island was rejected after G.M.Trevelyan had written to *The*

Times. The area to be devastated in Llŷn was one of the strongholds of Welsh language culture. When a language group is small and struggling to maintain its identity, the destruction of even one small flourishing community is intolerable to it. The old house that was pulled down by the service authorities exactly a week before Saunders Lewis and his two friends burnt down the aircraft sheds, had a place in Welsh history and Welsh literary history. The full details can be read in Saunders Lewis's speech in his own defence. The government that was responsible, he said, came down to a number of officials in the Air Ministry in London to whom Wales was no more than a name on the map.

This is always the trouble: there *are* two nations, there *are* two cultures. The English higher civil servant in the end belongs to the same culture as G.M. Trevelyan but not to the same culture as Saunders Lewis. The Penyberth case has been overtaken by a whole series of issues, often the drowning of Welsh valleys. The same passion on the one side and incomprehension on the other has been seen time and time again; but the power has been in the hands of those who have not understood.

A Government decision can be presented as democratic despite the protest of all shades of Welsh opinion, so long as the unit is thought of as the United Kingdom. Even if Welsh M.P.'s resist being dragooned by their party machine and protest as they did when Tryweryn was drowned, they are merely a handful in the House of Commons. The leaders of any protest, particularly if it becomes militant, are presented to everyone, including the Welsh people, as a few politically motivated fanatics; this is a pattern that has often been seen in colonial territories. But it is ignorance rather than malice that underlies these injustices, though this does not make things easier for the victims. In 1969 the same pattern could be observed when police brought in from England began to manhandle the student members of the Welsh Language Society who were protesting peacefully. There had been bomb explosions in Wales and the police were naturally jumpy. But they could not distinguish a movement which is intellectual, non-violent and has much in common with the tone of C.N.D. in England, from other sorts of Nationalist organization. Had C.N.D. marchers been treated as members of the Welsh Language Society were after a peaceful demonstration at the National Eisteddfod at Flint in 1969, Vanessa Redgrave would be camping on the steps of Scotland Yard, the producers and commentators on television would themselves be sympathetic, and the chief demonstrators would turn out to be the children of junior ministers in the government. But looked at from London, all Welsh demonstrators merge and are written off as nationalist extremists.

At Caernarfon, Saunders Lewis was able to appeal to a jury of Welshmen who *did* understand what the issues involved were. It is worth translating from his defence speech:

'I am a lecturer in Welsh literature at the University College of Swansea. That is my profession. It is also my chief pleasure and pride. Welsh literature is one of the most splendid literatures in Europe, the only direct descendant in these islands of the literary disciplines of classical antiquity. And it is a literature that is alive and growing, that draws sustenance from and grows out of a living spoken tongue and out of a social life that keeps its old traditions unbroken.

'It was realizing this direct connection between our literature and the traditional life of Welsh society that first drew me away from literature into public life and led me, with others, to form the Welsh Nationalist Party. . .

'What I was teaching the young people of Wales in the halls of the university was not a dead literature, something chiefly of interest to antiquarians, but the living literature of the Welsh people. This literature is therefore able to make demands of me as a man as well as a teacher.'

The appeal which Saunders Lewis went on to make was to the jury's moral sense, in the name of which he asked them to overturn a system of formalized law, by whose criteria they were clearly guilty. His defence was therefore a revolutionary one, very much as Castro's was at Moncada. It is not difficult to understand, after reading the quoted passage, why Saunders Lewis is an inspiration to Welsh students, who, like students everywhere, reject the isolation of academic life from the events of the time.

The jury at Caernarfon failed to agree on a verdict, and the case was transferred to the Old Bailey in London, where the accused were found guilty and sentenced. This tactical success for the British Government has turned out to be a great strategic mistake. The lesson, which only a few people learnt at first, but which more and more have come to understand with the passing of time, is that the forms of British democracy can be used to silence a minority when necessary.

An interesting and rather sad letter from Lloyd George to his daughter Megan has recently come to light. Lloyd George was already an old man by the time of Penyberth, and although it seems that he offered no help to the Nationalist leaders during the campaign against the bombing-school, this is what he wrote from Jamaica after hearing that the case had been transferred to the Old Bailey:

> They yield when faced by Hitler and Mussolini, but they attack the smallest country in the kingdom which they misgovern. This is a cowardly way of showing their strength through violence. . . This is the first government that has tried to put Wales on trial in the Old Bailey. . . I should like to be there, and I should like to be forty years younger.

But it is not a question of one particular Government. Although the accused in the Free Wales Army Trial of 1969 had a poorer case and were in every way immeasurably less worthy of respect than Saunders Lewis, the political cynicism with which they were treated was the same.

Before his second trial, that is to say before his conviction, Saunders Lewis was suspended from his duties as lecturer in the university college at Swansea. But during this same period Owen Parry of the Welsh BBC commissioned him to write a radio play for St.David's Day 1937.

This was a courageous and generous gesture. *Buchedd Garmon*, the play that Saunders Lewis wrote, was in verse, dealt with the time of the Pelagian heresy in early Wales, and while it is not to be seen as a direct political allegory of modern Wales, contains passages which are a kind of self-justification by the author; one in particular is now quoted up and down Wales at meetings of *Plaid Cymru* and other movements. It shows how creative and cherishing and positive Saunders Lewis's attitude to Wales is, and it can stand as the motto and explanation of the whole national movement in Wales, which came into being not to assert a political ambition but to defend a human and precious heritage. Emrys the King asks Bishop Garmon to accompany him to the battle.

> A certain man planted on a fruitful hillside
> A vineyard in which he set the best vines;
> He built a wall around it, raised a tower in the
> centre
> And gave it to his son as an inheritance
> To bear his name from generation to generation.
> But a herd of pigs broke down the wall of the
> vineyard,
> Rushed in to trample and eat up the vines.
> Is it not right that the son should stand in the
> breach now,

And call his friends to him, and protect his
inheritance?
My country of Wales is a vineyard, given into my
keeping,
To be handed down to my children and my
children's children
As an inheritance for all time.
And look, the pigs are rushing in to despoil it.
Therefore I now call upon all my friends,
The common man and the scholar,
Come to me now, stand with me in the breach
That the beauty of the past be kept for the times
that shall come.

There is a question that the English reader will have
asked himself several times in this book: if the Welsh
national movement has such a strong case, has suffered
much patent injustice, has had such able and persuasive
leaders, why is it not larger? Why has it not achieved
more? Part of the answer lies in the power of institutions,
some of which are discussed elsewhere in this book. But
also, and not separable from the power of institutions, is
the psychological aspect, and this in the end is what
is crucial.

The point has already been made in the chapter on the
language, that older Welsh-speakers often have an
ambivalence in their attitude to speaking Welsh. Just as
there are Welsh-speakers who can be found to jeer at the
demonstrations of the Welsh Language Society, so the
most emotional opposition to everything Welsh comes
from a certain type of Welshman. One can only conclude
that there is an ambivalence in the personality and that
Welsh people are often fighting something in themselves. Since deference to the English language, and to
the English in Wales, has for centuries been inseparable
from deference to the higher social class, there is some
plausibility in the theory that Welsh people do not grow
up with full confidence in their identity but to different
degrees awaken to it, and that the process of gaining con-

fidence, straightening the back and holding the head high is a painful one, and one that meets with some internal resistance, as with the awakening of a suppressed class or group anywhere.

Saunders Lewis is himself someone who discovered his Welshness. He was brought up in the Liverpool Welsh community and studied in the English department of the university there. Like so many Welsh people he had to find his Welsh background through his family, through literature, and through returning to Wales.

Implicit in Saunders Lewis's work, and accepted by many educated Welsh people, is the theory that as a nation we have become conditioned to servility, that we are afraid to be ourselves. Saunders Lewis appeals to and at the same time repels many Welsh people because he is asking them to cast out fear, to dare to be their true selves, to throw off their provincial innocence, their playing at being Welsh for their masters, and to take responsibility for themselves and for the future of their society and its culture. The challenge is not an overtly political one. The setting in his plays in not necessarily modern Wales, or Wales at all; it can be Eastern Europe or occupied France. But always his characters speak and act up to the full capacities and tragic limitations of human beings. 'Life,' says one of his characters, 'is a perilous gift given to us all'.

Because they think and feel in Welsh, his characters show what it means to be human in the Welsh mould. There *is* no universal human mould. Universality is always felt through the specific shapes which it takes in different times and places. And characters in fiction or drama do not merely derive from the types of people known to their creator; when they are great characters, they offer, through no conscious design of the author, a kind of model which helps to create the national culture. Natasha Rostov passed into Tolstoy's pages from something in his experience, but she was imagined so fully and endowed with such constructive beauty as a character, that she then passed back out into Russian life as a manner, gestures, aspirations, a way in which people could see themselves and others. So with some of Saunders Lewis's characters, particularly his women, who by their depth and decisiveness and spiritual courage challenge the audience to rise above itself: 'Iris's way of loving frightens me', says one of his weaker male characters: 'She loves me as if eternity existed'.

Saunders Lewis's treatment of love, while never trivial, is never puritanical. When Siwan, Llywelyn's queen, gives herself to her young lover, she knows the personal and political risks but does not overstate her emotions. 'Can't you love me, Siwan?' the young man asks, and she replies:

> 'I don't know yet; tonight it is enough to give myself.
> Tomorrow, who knows? Perhaps I shall love you tomorrow'.

Saunders Lewis has no place for a restrictive puritanism and indeed is bound to attack it insofar as it inhibits people's capacity, and the Welsh people's capacity for full humanity. This too is a subject that leads us back into politics, once we allow that Welsh politics is about a kind of self-liberation.

Welsh people who have read or sat through a performance of a Saunders Lewis play feel a heightened sense of their identity, of their potentiality. When they walk out on to the street in Wales, they are in a second-rate province of the English culture where trumpery heraldic notions of Welshness are fostered to flatter their self-esteem.

The whole situation, the very metaphors of awakening, of finding something which is hidden below a more superficial stratum, of overcoming fear, recall the world revolutionary movements. How often *they* speak of political awakening as being the pre-condition for political success, but at the same time insist that political action by the few is the precondition for that more general awakening.

The strength and danger of any revolutionary movement is that it is trying to express something that has not wholly come to the surface, and until it does we are asked to take the word of a few people that they represent the hope of the future. Fortunately there is another factor at work in Wales, as everywhere, alongside the theory of awakening and the ambivalence of many ordinary people: there are the circumstances and events of the time which in the end will not tolerate unreality in ideas or ambivalence in attitudes.

The revolution which Saunders Lewis offers Welsh people has a particular interest in terms of our tradition. It is both a call to change the social framework, and a call to change oneself, to cut away the layers of convention, the isolated and alienated and distorted self, to reveal the true self and the true Welsh self. We are speaking in almost religious terms, and this is not accidental. The great tradition in Welsh religion is one of self-searching. One of Saunders Lewis's main points about Pantycelyn is that he was a great doctor of souls. Religious *experience* was what counted for him. Whereas other men made their names as preachers in the Methodist movement in Wales, Pantycelyn's influence was through his hymns of experience and through helping to establish the *Seiat*.

The *Seiat*—or Society of Experience—was a meeting for public confession and self-criticism established in the days of early Methodism; it still exists, though institutionalized out of its former intensity. To Saunders Lewis, a convert to Roman Catholicism, the *Seiat* represented the instinctive groping of the Welsh religious mind towards the confessional which he sees as necessary for psychological health.

Not many Welsh people have followed Saunders Lewis into Catholicism. Many of the young people who are politically influenced by him would not claim to be religious at all. But the language of religious experience, with its metaphors of depth, of uncovering the true person, has adapted itself readily to the analysis of Welshness. And in the end it is perhaps not merely an analogy. To assert the value of a human community and the continuity of one's thoughts with those of one's ancestors, over the self-interested logic of administrators and profit-maximizers, *is* a kind of spiritual assertion.

Finally we come to the question of violence and to Saunders Lewis's expressed views on the subject. It is best to give a direct quotation from an interview:

> 'I personally believe that careful, considered, public violence is often a necessary weapon for national movements, necessary to defend the land, the valleys of Wales from being violated, wholly illegally, by the government and by the big corporations in England. I think, for instance, that Tryweryn, Clywedog, Cwm Dulas, are attacks that cannot be justified on moral grounds at all. The fact that they were decided on by the English Parliament confers no moral right. And so I think that any means that hinders this irresponsible violence on the land of Wales by English corporations, is wholly just.'
>
> 'Do you include the shedding of blood?'
>
> 'So long as it is Welsh blood and not English blood.'

This remark is a frightening one, but it is not the sign of an abnormal fanatical mind, as is sometimes suggested by his detractors. The majority of people have always believed that there are things which in certain circumstances it is worth dying for. Saunders Lewis has not advocated that the Welsh should initiate a campaign of violence as a means to achieve political independence; but he does say that one must be prepared, emotionally prepared, for a struggle more bitter than a constitutional one, that one cannot expect justice and that resisting injustice may lead to loss of life.

He looks with head-shaking pity at the easy hopes of *Plaid Cymru*. How nice it would be if everything were to come about constitutionally, with London handing over power to Cardiff as soon as a simple majority of Welsh seats fell to the Nationalists. I am not myself convinced that this would happen. There are no constitutional precedents and it is quite possible that a London government would invent criteria for secession which disregarded the expressed will of a majority in Wales.

But much more to the point than this hypothesis is the view of Wales as a place where democracy is formalized, where a constitutional nationalist party cannot hope to win. An electoral setback for *Plaid Cymru* will, for some of its adherents, reinforce the feeling that what we have is a revolutionary situation, requiring revolutionary action, if only to the extent of massive non-violent direct-action. In other words, many people hope with Gwynfor Evans and doubt with Saunders Lewis. There is always a tension between evolutionary and revolutionary views of change. Saunders Lewis from time to time criticized the leadership of *Plaid Cymru* for *naïveté*, and as often *Plaid Cymru* leaders repudiated his views; both sides acting in good faith. But seen from outside the two strains in Welsh nationalism are complementary. One concentrates on constitutional planning, organization, the superficial but necessary processes by which votes are won and movements consolidated, and draws in the people who are interested in politics at this level. The other strain is deeper, prepares for a long struggle, perhaps for suffering. It will never win a great number of votes, but it has the depth and richness which give the activists the strength they need in all movements to persevere and endure to the end. Asked in 1968 how he saw the future, Saunders Lewis refused to predict anything, and added:

'I don't think anyone should join any movement, even a movement to save the nation, just because they hope—or are sure—that it will be successful. I should remain committed to Wales even if I were certain that within ten years Wales would be finished. The only thing I would say would be that the world and Wales would be poorer. The fact that evil triumphs doesn't prove that evil is good. Can we leave it at that?'

6 / The Chains around my Feet

WHEREVER YOU look in the modern Welsh culture you find the word 'remember'. It is there in Gwenallt and Saunders Lewis and in the songs of Dafydd Iwan. It is there too in the slogans painted on walls and bridges: *Cofia Tryweryn*—'Remember Tryweryn', the most notorious case of a Welsh valley drowned despite the general protest of Wales; and more recently *Cofia Abergele*, the place where the two deaths took place on the morning of the Investiture.

This is not an antiquarian sort of remembering; it is remembering who you are, where you come from, what has happened to you and your people. In a country where so few outward things tell you that you are Welsh it adds a quality of depth to the consciousness, a pole of resistance to the constant suggestion that we should forget and be content and, above all, consume.

Even the landscape takes on a different quality if you are one of those who remembers. The scenery is then never separate from the history of the place, from the feeling for the lives that have been lived there. The great quarry tips of Caernarfonshire stand both as evidence and image of the hardship of the past. In the Cardiganshire countryside you have the pattern of whitewashed smallholders' cottages against the rolling green fields; in the South the bare mountain stretches free above the huddled mining village and coal tip. Always the outlines of the scenery are deep in the Welsh consciousness as if scored in thick paint on canvas. But one only knows this quality of depth through reading, in history and literature, about the past, feeling it as it has been felt by those who have lived Welsh history within that landscape. All the time the Welsh have to assert this feeling for Wales against the way of looking from outside that sees it as a picturesque view, or, more recently, as recreational space.

Those who forget become another bit of flotsam on the tide of industrial society, with no way of looking at themselves except as members of some functional category, their anxieties and insecurities played on by the commercial culture. But those persons who remember also run a risk of becoming negative and embittered. To remember the Welsh past is to remember, very largely, hardship and poverty and injustice, and these are things that it is human to want to escape from and forget as soon as you can. This then is the dilemma—and it is one that can be paralleled elsewhere: how do we emerge from the rich and human cultures, which were nevertheless cultures of scarcity and hardship, without sacrificing our humanity to the machine that has been our deliverance?

I can never read Kate Roberts' first novel *Traed mewn Cyffion* (The Chains around my Feet) without feeling that it explains, in a way that is very close to me, the continuous social experience in which the generations of my parents and grandparents were caught up, the generations that escaped from poverty but still face the dilemma of their Welshness.

Part of the closeness derives from the fact that the novel is set in Caernarfonshire, and that the conversations are written in a dialect not very different from that of my mother, whose Welsh has passed to me. Kate Roberts (whose greatest achievement, it is only fair to say in passing, is probably in the short story) is writing about a quarrying village near Caernarfon, higher up towards the mountains than the town itself, looking down to the Norman castle and the town, and west to the long arm of the Llŷn peninsula. The story begins in 1880 when Ifan and Jane Gruffydd are newly married. We see Jane's moments of pride as a young wife, the time, before the routine of housework and children wipe everything else from her mind, when she becomes aware of herself as an individual mysteriously existing in this particular time and place. It is the catching of these moments, often in childhood or old age, that Kate Roberts is perhaps best at, but this novel also shows the social forces converging on the domestic situation, and for the moment it is here that our chief interest lies. Through Ifan we learn about the system of contract employment at the quarry, the scope it gave for bribing officials, and victimizing particular workmen. We learn, from the experience of one family, how illness meant the descent from simple poverty into poverty racked with worry and debts. Death strikes suddenly at the quarry face. The quarry-owners are far away, and English, and automatically hated. The union is just beginning to gather membership.

But this is not a novel that depresses one. We are taken into the world of the children as they grow up, the expeditions for bilberries, the gathering of heather to kindle the fire. The quarry is only one source of the family's income, and they help to keep themselves alive by farming a smallholding. This gives the beauty of a rural environment to their lives even when these are beset by poverty. The happiness of the children convinces precisely because it is set in contrast to the hardship of adult life, and very soon the children, too, come to appreciate the meaning of poverty through some small incident affecting their lives. This is very far from the picturesque world of some Anglo-Welsh writing, in which Wales has become the prelapsarian childhood land, where children are forever eating home-made scones before warm fires while kindly grandmothers scurry around the sanded slate floor. As with attitudes to the landscape, so here we have to beware of turning our past into a place peopled by folk figures.

Owen is the first of the children to win a scholarship to the secondary school. Even so it will cost money and there is some doubt whether the family will be able to afford the loss of earnings which he would otherwise bring home from the quarry. But like so many Welsh families of the period, his family does all that is humanly possible to send him on. Education is something honoured in itself, but it is also the escape from poverty.

The entry of the working-class to higher education in fair numbers happened earlier in Wales than in England, and the tensions created by this experience occur—with Welsh variations—earlier in our literature. Owen's years at school and later as a university student produce many of the emotions found in post-Second World War English literature (Kate Roberts' novel was published in 1936). The values of education are something alien, and the boy who walks morning and evening between school and the warmth of his home moves between two quite different worlds of value. Through education Owen makes his way into what promises to be an easier life; his parents wish this for him, and yet he feels a strong attachment to the world of his parents and a guilt at the sacrifice made to set him on his way. He is appalled by the deference his parents show to the educated world which he knows to be no better, indeed finds less worthy of respect than they themselves are.

'Escaping from poverty, that's what we've been doing all the time,' Twm, another brother who goes to college, tells Owen. Even the move to take up quarrying in an earlier generation had been made to get away from the greater poverty on the land. Now Owen and his brother

Twm escape through education. Wiliam, the third brother, leaves the quarries for the mines of the South. This, too, is an escape, for wages are higher there and the unions are better organized. Sioned, one of the daughters, moves out of poverty in a different way. Early on she discovers that a girl with her looks can find an easier life for herself. She marries a shop-assistant in the town and moves into a wholly different culture where people live in hopes of winning newspaper competitions, and where aspirations are largely those created by advertising and the commercialized fashions of the time. The new son-in-law shows in his character and manners the creeping influence of the industrial mass-culture, and this is registered very subtly by the degree of anglicization in his character and language. He has nothing to talk about with his in-laws whose life has been much harder but less demeaning, a life lived seriously, not trivially. Once more we are brought up against the dilemma that the release from hardship has given individuals a chance to develop, but that the machines of production and mass-communication want to control our new power to choose for ourselves. The forces that make us economically more equal and classless are not entirely democratic forces.

Sioned's husband later abandons her, and during the First World War she takes up with various army officers who are posted to the area. Her break with the traditional morality is also a kind of escape from hardship. Indeed the puritan rectitude of her parents is to be seen as part of the culture of hardship. They live thriftily not because of some twisted religious principle but because that is the only way to stay alive and keep some control over your own future.

The phenomenon we have been dealing with has been that of the social emergence of a class from a situation of poverty and injustice. But people do not suffer and do not emerge in merely economic terms. These people were a class but they were also Welsh, and the Welsh variants in the situation now have to be mentioned.

From the start at school Owen is aware that education is a process of alienating him from his background, and from his *Welsh* background, because he has to write everything in English, get his tongue round English words to speak to the teachers. When he wins prizes on one occasion, his mother declines to come to the prize-giving because she doesn't understand a word of English. In the end the process of education comes to alienate Owen from society as it is, rather than to alienate him from his family, and in this he is rather different from the working-class boy going through higher education in English literature.

The war, when it comes, is again a form of escape. Twm joins up, not through any patriotic feeling but because the education system, in which he is now a teacher, is so repressive. He is bullied by his head-master, and he is not allowed to teach Welsh, one of the subjects in which he has taken his degree. Always the injustice to the Welsh identity is mixed in with the general injustice, and so it is when the greatest blow of all falls on the family.

They have never believed that Twm will be sent overseas. Now they hear that he is in France, and soon an official letter arrives. It is, of course, in English; Jane Gruffydd, who is at home when the postman comes, takes it down to the village for the grocer to translate, thinking it is some form to be filled in about the smallholding. It is the news of Twm's death, and when Ifan, out helping a neighbour with the hay, sees a man crossing the field to call him home, he does not need to be told what has happened. Later Owen thinks to himself that in war it isn't only the killing and the suffering that is cruel, but the incidental things like this. His mother had to get someone to *translate* the news of her son's death.

The chapter which contains these two incidents, told with the spare stoicism of Hemingway at his best, captures the terrible helplessness of ordinary people everywhere in the face of power over which they have no control, and stands in my mind alongside the passage in Bernanos' *Les Grands Cimetières sous la Lune* where the men in Majorca, coming in from their day's work in the fields, are, during the Spanish Civil War, taken off to their deaths in army lorries, leaving the soup to get cold on the table set for their meal.

This same chapter shows Kate Roberts at her most passionate:

> Things had been bad with them before. They had suffered injustice in the quarries, the oppression of officials and owners, bribery and favouritism. They had seen their friends and children killed at work, but they had never seen their children taken away from them to be killed in war. . . They did not believe any longer that the purpose of the war was to defend small nations, and that it was a war to end wars; they did not believe that one country was more to blame than another. . .

In this passage we see, alongside the crystallizing anger of an exploited class, the dissociation of a minority nation from the political aims of the State. I remember it again from my own childhood during the Second World War. The identification with the war effort among my own relatives in North Wales was certainly much weaker than in Britain generally. We were all against Hitler, of course, but no one was going to have their children called up if they could do anything to stop it. The distance between *them* and *us* is multiplied when *they* belong to another nation.

Thinking back to that time I can begin to understand the dilemma of suppressed minorities in Nazi-occupied

Europe. The Slovaks collaborated and were given their own puppet-state; some Bretons and some Ukrainians welcomed the invaders too, though eventually among all these nationalities the Germans produced a reaction against themselves, leaving the national movements in each country split after the war into a left-wing and a right-wing. Wales has fortunately avoided this split, but the fundamental situation in which the suppressed group stands aside from the sense of purpose of the imposed central state, is one that we still have. Sometimes the British state is directly hostile to our separate life as Welsh, sometimes it can be manipulated in our favour, but it never belongs to us. Old-style capitalism is replaced by a mixture of capitalism and state socialism, some things improve, but there is never complete justice because as Welsh we are not given the rights the English have as English.

After his brother's death, Owen's resolve hardens, as Kate Roberts' own must have when her brother was killed in the same war:

> His eyes were opened to the possibility of *doing* something, instead of suffering mutely. It was high time for someone to stand up to all this injustice, and to do something. This was the weakness of his own people; they had a heroic capacity for suffering, but it did not extend to acting against the cause of that suffering.

In that generation a great many Welsh people stood up against the injustice by joining the Labour movement and helped to remove many of the economic injustices. But a few people, while still opposing economic injustice, also opposed the injustice to us as Welsh people, and Kate Roberts was one of these. All her life she has worked for *Plaid Cymru*, and for many years ran with her husband the Welsh weekly *Baner ac Amserau Cymru*, a publication which, in those days, survived by constantly asking for donations from its readers and getting them.

In its early days Welsh nationalism certainly concentrated too much on cultural questions, and with time it has come to understand the way these interrelate with economics. Nevertheless there *is* some basis for the assertion that, at least among Welsh-speakers, nationalism represents a chiefly cultural discontent. To some people this means that it is therefore a secondary discontent.

But by today the main socialist criticisms of society *are* cultural in the broadest sense; they concern the quality of life and the right to participate, rather than sheer economic inequalities. A good society is seen to be one that not merely guarantees certain wage levels but makes the material and cultural environment fit to live in. Criticism of the mass-media, of institutional structure, of advertising, is criticism from a cultural angle, which is not to deny that these phenomena too have an economic base. To depreciate cultural criticism of society and to maintain that only crude economic injustices are worth calling injustice, is oneself to be tied to notions born in times of hardship and scarcity.

The argument that only wages and material conditions matter is by today a conservative argument. These need to be kept at a certain level anyway for the proper functioning of the system of consumption and production. We need to move on from talking of 'emergence' which is a negative concept, to the concept of the 'entry into society' of a given group or class. By this I understand a situation in which the group feel confident that its own values and beliefs can contribute to the making of the future.

Like the English, the Welsh have emerged from hardship. It is a process that leaves people exhausted and often content for a time merely to enjoy the freedom from want. But the full entry of the Welsh into society is still barred. They can only get in by leaving their Welshness behind them. They do not share all the assumptions, the conventions which even the different classes of English have in common, their tensions are different ones, they bring with them another language and until they can have the conditions for the free working out of this inheritance, they can never enter fully as Welsh into the larger human society.

7 / D.J.

I AM glad that I came back to Wales in time to have met D.J.Williams (known as D.J.) who died in January 1970; otherwise I should have suspected that the legend could not be true.

It is a legend of purity of heart, of complete disinterestedness, of a man who for nearly half a century sacrificed most of his working hours, and some would say his literary talent, to *Plaid Cymru*, which he joined in its earliest days. There are endless stories of his humour on the platform or canvassing on doorsteps and in pubs; he was always selling party literature, writing letters to newspapers, starting up conversations in trains and aiming with wit and good-humour to persuade. It was he who joined with Saunders Lewis and Lewis Valentine in burning down the bombing-sheds at Penyberth and found he had got his matches damp; and who later at the police-station was heard discussing Williams-Parry's sonnets with his colleagues; who *liked* prison because of the characters he found there, and particularly the Jewish prisoners whose sense of humour he shared. He was always fond of company and of the pub; indeed he lived in a former pub, the old *Bristol Trader* in Fishguard.

But what most fixed the legend of D.J. was the selling of the old family farmhouse, Penrhiw, and the donation of the money to *Plaid Cymru*. This sum of £2,000 was the most the party had ever received, though when 'D.J.' died, more than this was given within a few days to *Plaid Cymru* in tribute to him.

His death too was legendary. He had gone to give an address at a concert in Rhydcymerau, the village where he was brought up. The concert was in the chapel which he had attended as a boy. After making his speech he returned to his seat and died. On the day after his death, everyone I met had some memory of him, something to say. An old lady whom I met on the street and who was his contemporary, said 'What a rounded life', and a group of students recalled him during an election campaign in Pembrokeshire. They had been canvassing all day for *Plaid Cymru* and in the evening were relaxing in the pub. At about 9 o'clock the figure of D.J. appeared; he had just stopped canvassing from door to door and proceeded to sell party literature round the bar.

Not very long before his death D.J. had attended the trial of some members of the Welsh Language Society at Cardigan. Dafydd Iwan recalls the occasion:

> At the end of the trial, when things were looking pretty black, I felt a firm hand on my arm, and D.J.'s voice saying: "Don't worry, Dafy *bach*, though we lose today, there's always tomorrow". I shall feel that hand and hear those words as long as I live.

I only met D.J. twice, and that in the last year of his life. It was enough to give me that sense of essential and simple goodness that one encounters very rarely. With his shining rounded face and small glittering eyes he reminded me of a robin. His optimism, the simple belief that Wales was at last emerging from centuries of silent oppression, seemed naïve even to some people within the party which in his last years had to concern itself with planning and research and organization on a more impersonal scale than was known in the early days. But in this naïveté there was also a kind of greatness. Struggling minority movements are particularly open to factionalism and rancour. They need figures of this kind, and D.J.'s wholeheartedness and purity of intention must have been of immense value in uniting the party.

But there is something else very important in the figure of D.J. He was naturally Welsh as a tree is naturally green; he never doubted his identity. Enough has been written in this book to suggest that to be Welsh is very often to have a torn or split consciousness, to have to *discover* your background, to *will* your identity, to separate underlying from superficial levels in your personality. The committed Welshman is very often a deep introspective kind of person, who has gained an inner strength at the expense of withdrawal from the ordinary non-political life of everyday, and who cannot but feel a kind of personal bitterness at the circumstances in which we have to live as Welsh people. But D.J. stands as a pole of positive attraction, someone perfectly sure of himself, the best kind of Welsh personality, produced, as it were, in the natural state. The words he applied to one of the characters of his childhood are also appropriate to him: 'He was a man living in a warm, close-knit society, and that warmth was enough to keep him happy and cosy to the end of his life.'

D.J.'s background is described in a number of short stories, character-sketches and autobiographical books, the most famous of which, *Hen Dŷ Ffarm* (The Old Farmhouse), has been translated into English. It is a very difficult book to translate adequately precisely because it *does* deal with so wholly Welsh a background.

The same difficulty arises when it comes to interpreting D.J. to a non-Welsh public. He was a good writer but not one who transcended the limits of his own national culture. He relied more on colloquial turns of phrase, a characteristic brand of humour, than on ideas, which are more easily translated. Though politically dedicated he did not break new ground in his thinking. He was a 'character', yet even as I write that I know that this will be taken in a picturesque and old-fashioned sense. More than with any other writer dealt with in this book I have to ask the reader to take my word for what he means to us, for the sense of staunchness and rock-like conviction, mixed with gaiety, which he gave in his person and in the best of his writings. The foreign, and especially the urban reader, needs a particularly long leap of sympathy to understand the attraction of D.J.—though a meeting would have established it immediately.

D.J. came of a farming family in north Carmarthenshire, the same area that Gwenallt visited on holiday from the industrial south (indeed the two families were related). The society in which he was brought up must have changed less in several centuries than it has since D.J. left. It was a virtually monoglot Welsh community, though there was English for those who went to school, and in the remote big houses of the neighbourhood. Carmarthen town with its English law court was further away psychologically than it was geographically and D.J. as a child absorbed a feeling that it was alien, something he later saw as a kind of superstition going back to the time when the ordinary Welsh people in the countryside looked with distrust towards the Norman castle.

Within itself the Welsh community was rich, warm and highly differentiated. In *Hen Dŷ Ffarm* humans and animals are very close to each other; animals too have distinct characters. D.J.'s people are fine specimens of a type and whatever they do they do well, rather as characters in Chaucer do. Dialect is used for its warm expressiveness rather than to draw attention or for picturesque effect. Everyone in the community is joined to everyone else by a mesh of stories and incidents if not by family relationships. Quite long stretches of the book are in fact taken up with the tracing of family connections. The urge to keep hold of one's family history D.J. saw as part of a valuable instinct to hold the present and the past together, the process which makes civilization possible.

Hen Dŷ Ffarm is chiefly concerned with his life up to the age of six, and in one famous passage D.J. speaks of the 'square mile' in which the child first learns everything which is of real importance. This experience was at the root of his own nationalism. Long before he went to school he learnt history and geography from his mother who told him about the people they met, the names of trees and streams and particular fields; and here too he absorbed the values of the society:

> Here, in this simple home, were stowed away my notions about religion, about education, about my country, about language and about life, before these abstract terms meant anything to my understanding. It was a matter of atmosphere and tradition that came down from generation to generation.

His account of his own background is much subtler than descriptions that are sometimes given of 'the Welsh way of life'. There were chapels and *eisteddfodau* in the society in which he was reared, but they play only a small part in his description and are subservient to pheasants and horses and pubs and stories and singers. One must always beware of those institutions which a society holds up as its highest achievement. Apart from the fact that 'national values' are usually the values projected by the most powerful and dominant section of the community, anything that is made explicitly a 'value' is probably in a state of fossilization. It is the assumptions of the society, what it does *not* make explicit, that in the end are perhaps the deepest influences. Or in D.J.'s own words:

> It's as impossible to define another national way of life as to define the smell of flowers. You see the flowers, and you know the difference between the smell of one and another. Nations are the same. There is a flavour in a particular society that you

don't get in the others.

D.J.Williams was one of the generation that was propelled out of a way of life that had been continuous for centuries into the restless world we know. Education shot him into a new sphere of consciousness and he was able to turn, as it were, and sum up, before it disappeared, the richness of life and the density of texture in the traditional culture. This is what lends a memorable and static quality to some of his descriptions, as if he intends to fix things for ever in his memory and ours:

> But these cows come oftenest to mind not seen in the cowshed in the dark of winter, but leisurely chewing the cud in the farmyard on a warm summer day with two or three milking-women pulling at their udders; and near them but a little to one side, the bull standing like a Roman idol, his thoughtful spittle dropping to the ground in a silver thread.

D.J.'s departure from the traditional culture takes the form of a symbolic incident. On Christmas mornings the men in the family would go out shooting, and this particular Christmas, having found little to shoot at, he took two guns, one in each hand, held them up in the air and fired them simultaneously for the fun of it:

> This was the last Christmas before I left home for the first time—never to return as a full citizen. The previous June I had had my sixteenth birthday, and on the fourth of January I was going to work to Glamorganshire. . . With those two reckless shots, I took, unknown to myself, the last fling of my unspoilt rural life, the life I have loved so much in retrospect across the years. I believe I was the first ever, of all my line, to leave the land.

Those gunshots mark a moment in a process that could be paralleled right across Europe. It is happening now in northern Russia where the magnificent carved wooden houses of Archangel province stand empty as the young make for the cities, and in the mountain villages of

Castile where every family has menfolk working in France or Germany. And everywhere the accumulated tradition of centuries yields to the culture of television and plastic.

The choice is not between keeping things as they were or changing them—*that* choice does not exist—but between abandoning the past or taking responsibility for the transmission of its values. In the conditions of Wales the second choice is the nationalist choice. D.J. Williams registers the Welsh culture at the time it changes from being a culture of localities to being a national political consciousness. 'Up to the age of 26, my experience was particular to me. After that it moved into the stream of nationalism.'

When D.J. speaks of his own family and its farmland, his own attitude to the diminishing material inheritance and his growing responsibility for the social inheritance, he might be speaking for the national movement generally:

> Territorially, my family's inheritance has got smaller over the centuries, until it has almost vanished entirely in my own time. But this has never worried me in the least, since I feel that I have somehow been allowed to keep something that is dearer in my sight than land or possessions—namely the consciousness of the ancient values of our fathers, together with a feeling of responsibility for their continuance. There is, in this feeling, a touch of Welsh citizenship that has not been killed by long oppression and violence, something that wholly unfits me to be a loyal citizen to any other authority. All loyalty is false that is not based on consent and on moral justice.

It is sometimes said that D.J. Williams would have been a greater writer if he could have foregone making political points. One can agree that he sometimes made them too obviously and predictably, and yet defend the political tendency as inseparable from his merits. With his background, what alternative did a writer have? He could have ignored the background, he could have treated it as picturesque antiquarian's material; but he chose to treat it responsibly, asking how the values of the society he had known as good could be transmitted to the future. He came to the conclusion that without some form of self-government Welsh people would never be able to protect and develop their moral and material resources. Near Rhydcymerau, where D.J. was reared, the land, improved by the labour of centuries, and now sold by English landlords to the British Forestry Commission and grown over with trees, reinforces his conclusion.

8 / Cymdeithas Yr Iaith

I HAVE already touched on *Cymdeithas yr Iaith Gymraeg* (The Welsh Language Society) in the chapter on Saunders Lewis. His radio lecture *Tynged yr Iaith* was the theoretical starting-point, and the Beasley family, cited by him, was the prototype of civil disobedience in the name of the language. But something must also be said about a nineteenth-century forerunner, Emrys ap Iwan, whose selected writings are now studied in sixth forms as well as in Welsh university courses.

At a time when Welsh was still reasonably secure, Emrys ap Iwan saw the necessity of making it once more an official language and the language of education if it was to survive. He campaigned against the anglicizing of Welsh place-names and dreamt of a movement of young people that would insist on using Welsh for all purposes in Wales, in council chamber and court of justice, in shops and commercial life; they would refuse to accept bills in English and would destroy or ignore English signs and notices. Had such a movement arisen in his own time when the majority of Welsh people were Welsh-speaking, many of them virtually monoglot Welsh, it could have been tremendously effective. By today, when the Welsh Language Society has come into being, English and Welsh-speakers live side by side throughout Wales (the latter in a minority) and although the Society hopes eventually to re-establish Welsh through the teaching of the language, its campaigns have never been against English as such, but to get Welsh put alongside English. They have asked for bilingual signs and documents, for the right to use Welsh as well as English in dealing with official authority. In view of statements made about the Society ('a minority trying to impose the language') this is a point to be kept constantly in mind.

Like Saunders Lewis, Emrys ap Iwan had a European perspective on Wales. He had spent some time in France and been influenced by the stylist and pamphleteer Paul-Louis Courier. Back in Wales he was able to stand apart from the provincial movement for 'getting-on' through English among the rising Welsh middle-class, and to appreciate that they were losing much more than they were gaining. Spending some time abroad, or with a foreign literature, is a sure way of making the Welsh more conscious of their own Welsh identity. It helps them separate out what in their background is distinct from the English culture. Education and travel do not make the Welsh less concerned with their own tradition but more aware of it. The Welsh movements are an alliance between an intelligentsia and ordinary, unassuming Welsh-speakers, who know in their bones what educated people know with their minds. In between come those who are 'making their way' necessarily through English. These, the *crachach* (an expressive word, equivalent to 'scabs' but outside the industrial sphere) are scorned by the other two groups.

This background helps one to understand why the Welsh Language Society attracts the most intelligent Welsh-speakers at the universities and in the sixth-forms. Labour M.P.'s in Wales have maintained that they are young people misled by a few old men such as Saunders Lewis. This is an old cry, that the teacher is corrupting the young (one thinks of Socrates) and it is always ineffective because it starts by insulting the intelligence and judgement of the young. A much more plausible explanation of the phenomenon of the Welsh Language Society is that it has been produced by the higher level of education.

The first protest occurred in 1963 when a member was caught giving his girl-friend a lift home on the cross-bar of his bike, and decided he had a right to a summons in Welsh. This was not available at that time, and from this incident developed the first demonstration—a sit-down in the road at Aberystwyth. There followed campaigns to get the Post Office to use Welsh outside and inside its buildings, to obtain various other documents in Welsh, and to register births in Welsh. A number of individuals made gestures that have passed into the history of the movement. Sali Davies refused to draw her old-age pension because the authorities would not provide her with forms in Welsh; a young man, Robat Gruffudd, now a printer and publisher of Welsh books, refused to accept his degree from the university college at Bangor because throughout his time there the college authorities had refused requests from Welsh students to have their language given equal treatment. In May 1966, the first of many members of the Society was imprisoned.

1967 saw the passing of the Welsh Language Act. This was claimed by the Government as a great achievement for the language. This promised something called 'equal validity' for the two languages. To the administrator this was something quite different from bilingualism, and so it turned out to be. But a lot of people thought that it meant Welsh alongside English notices and in public life generally. When this was found not to be the case campaigning became more vigorous.

It is true that you can now plead in Welsh in the courts; that many official forms are available in Welsh or bilingual versions; that you can receive income-tax forms and make the returns in Welsh; that you can write to Government departments and usually receive a reply in Welsh. But the British Government has acquired no merit in all this because it has always acted late, grudgingly, and as if its concern were to make the minimum concession rather than to transform the administration of Wales which is what giving Welsh equal treatment would really mean.

Thus, many official forms are available in alternative Welsh versions, but they have to be asked for specially. The educated Welsh-speaker who could well complete the form in English may ask or send for the Welsh version on principle (which the administration sees as a kind of cussedness) but ordinary Welsh-speakers may not know that the form now exists in Welsh, or if money (say a rating assessment) is involved, will think that by sending for a special form they draw attention to themselves. This does not mean that they would not prefer to deal in Welsh with the authorities. In the farming community in which I live (a rural district where 3000 of the 3600 population were Welsh-speaking in the 1961 census) I have had to discuss in Welsh with my neighbours the English forms coming through the post, and then helped to complete them in English.

There is really no fair alternative to the automatic provision of bilingual forms, or else of Welsh forms in the first place, in Welsh-speaking areas, which areas could be defined and redefined at regular intervals as are the Swedish-speaking parts of Finland. Sometimes in Wales, bureaucratic indifference seems to give way to bureaucratic malice, when one discovers, for instance, that certain forms are available in Welsh on request at the Post Office counter, but are specifically not on display by instruction of the Government department issuing the form. In these circumstances the low figures produced with glee by the Government as evidence of the small demand for Welsh forms, appear as sheer propaganda against the language. The real division is not between people who speak or do not speak the language, but between those who have the will to make bilingualism succeed, and those who make what concessions they have to but lack the imagination to envisage anything basically different from the present situation.

Everywhere direct action is the child of bureaucracy. It is produced by the realization that however strong your case, however reasonable your approach, you will be ignored or fobbed off with technical objections. This is what happened in Wales. The Welsh Language Society only acted after it had written to Government departments and received what it considered unsatisfactory replies. Moreover, it has managed to keep itself non-violent, perhaps because of its relatively small size and the cohesion of the group which does not attract outside hangers-on who do not share its aims.

One of the most successful early campaigns in terms of publicity for their case was the road-signs campaign of 1969. Members painted out a high proportion of the English road-signs throughout Wales, avoiding the kind of obliteration that would cause a hazard. Many of the signs were place-names which exist in an English and a Welsh version: thus Swansea is Abertawe, and Cardigan, Aberteifi. In Welsh-speaking areas (where the latter example occurs) the present situation is particularly ridiculous, since Aberteifi, the name used for miles in the countryside around, never appears on the signs. One has to imagine driving from Dover to London past signs marked only Douvres and Londres.

The first objection raised by the Welsh Office and the Ministry of Transport was that bilingual signs would be dangerous. When numerous foreign examples had been brought to dispose of the argument, we were asked to think of the expense, and to calculate the number of kidney-machines or hospitals or schools or houses that could be built with the money which a change to bilingual signs would involve. As it happened, very considerable sums of money had been spent on new monolingual signs between the time of the first requests by the Welsh Language Society and the production of this argument.

The road-signs campaign was one that no one in Wales could be unaware of. The public outside Wales became aware of the Society in 1969 because of its opposition to the Investiture of the Prince of Wales, and the satirical pop-song about the prince composed and sung by the Society's chairman, Dafydd Iwan. Further demonstrations at the 1969 National Eisteddfod received considerable publicity, again because the Prince was involved, and by early 1970 when Dafydd Iwan was himself imprisoned and young Welsh demonstrators invaded the High Court in London, most people in Britain and many abroad had a vague idea that there was a new young protest movement in Wales.

The publicity received by the Society was further evidence of the centralized nature of the press and mass-media. By taking advantage of the interest in the Prince and the Investiture in 1969, and by invading a court in London in 1970, the Society's members attracted more attention to their case than by endless demonstrations in Wales. What the British public saw was a mere fraction of the protest in Wales. Thus in the fortnight between 15th January and 30th January 1970, when Dafydd Iwan was in prison, fourteen demonstrations were held in different parts of Wales, many of which involved the occupation of magistrates' courts and other public buildings. The period 1969-70 also saw numerous hunger strikes, prison sentences and the occupation of BBC studios.

One question that arises in the case of every militant group is this: how representative is it? Early on, the Welsh Language Society was classified as a handful of extremists by the authorities in Wales and by the provincial English-language press, on which the London press usually relies for reports of what is happening here. Their activities were hardly ever described without the use of words such as 'vandals' and 'daubing' and their case was, generally speaking, kept out of the English-language press in Wales as an editor might keep out flat-earthers or other bodies regarded as a lunatic fringe.

Certainly the Society was unrepresentative of the majority of Welsh-speakers in its militancy. It came into existence to stand up for the language in a way previous generations had been unwilling to do, and a lot of people were shocked initially by the way young people sat down in the road, painted road-signs and so on. The remarkable thing is how with time the Society has got its message across to larger numbers of people.

The active membership of the Society consists mainly of students, and the total membership is said to be some thousand people. This is small only by the standards of the British community. If we judge it in relation to a total of 650,000 Welsh-speakers in Wales, this represents a proportion equal in British terms to something approaching a hundred thousand.

The Society has never been without wider support for its aims. Very often it has only demanded militantly what representative bodies have asked for constitutionally and unsuccessfully. Thus when 200 members of the Society sat down in front of the Post Office in Dolgellau in 1965 they were supporting a request by the town council for the new Post Office building to carry the word for Post Office in Welsh, a request that was then, and twice subsequently refused. The campaign for bilingual road-signs was merely demanding through direct action what Cardiganshire County Council had asked for in a letter to the Welsh Office, unsuccessfully.

But the campaigns of 1969-1970 turned support for the

aims into tacit and sometimes active support of the *methods* of the demonstrators. Older members of the Welsh community were forced either to align themselves with or to come out against the young people. When students came up for trial before justices of the peace for offences connected with the language, they usually admitted their technical guilt but took the opportunity to put their moral case; the reaction of magistrates was erratic, and the sentencing very uneven. Some magistrates discharged the accused on the spot, others imposed very severe fines. On one remarkable occasion the chairman of a bench in North Wales told the accused that while they must be found guilty, it was the court rather than they that were on trial that day. When Dafydd Iwan was in prison, twenty magistrates contributed to a fund set up to pay his fine and secure his release. There are policemen too who have been worried by the tension which bad administration creates between the demands of law and justice.

In the summer of 1969 a campaign was launched by the editor of the Welsh monthly *Barn* to see if he could get established Welsh figures to support an initiative of the Welsh Language Society. This was the campaign to get a bilingual road licence disc, a symbolic thing, which was seen as a test of the Government's intention to carry out what many people understood was the intention of the Welsh Language Act of 1967. The Ministry of Transport and the Welsh Office maintained that on a number of technical grounds, involving the ever-present excuse of the computer, bilingual licence discs could not be contemplated. *Barn* collected signatures from people who announced that they would not display monolingual licence discs after 1st September 1970, unless a promise of bilingual ones was forthcoming. When this list had reached a number of over 600, and included many well-known writers, university professors, and people eminent in various other fields, the authorities declared that the technical difficulties had been overcome, and the bilingual disc is now in use. The whole story is a kind of bureaucratic farce, but it also illustrates how something initiated by young demonstraters drew older and more respectable Welshmen into the field of direct atction.

The demonstration at the time of Dafydd Iwan's imprisonment showed very clearly the cohesion of the Welsh-speaking community. There was no generation gap, and the educated Welsh community was solidly behind the young demonstrators. Only people whose jobs required them to make noises of disapproval, did so. This included most of the Welsh M.P.s.

But the Welsh Language Society has been able to draw support outside its own ranks not only from among the educated community who understand the issues, but among young people who are not as educated as the students themselves. This it has done through pop-song.

The rise of Welsh pop is an interesting phenomenon that has been much discussed in Wales. It was made possible by the coincidence of a number of circumstances. A record can be marginally profitable without a very large market, and in Welsh broadcasting, always on the look-out for novelty in the Welsh culture, there existed the means to publicize the new songs. But equally important was the rise of a new kind of song.

'Pop' is a word that offers only a very rough equivalent for the new song in Wales. At its worst, Welsh pop is imitative of rather old-fashioned melody-styles (to sell well it has to appeal right across the generations) with naïve and sentimental lyrics; at its best it is satirical or political song running very close to Welsh reality and comparable with the Russian satirical songs of Galich or Vysotsky rather than anything one finds in England. The master of this genre is Dafydd Iwan.

In his songs the important things are the words, and the *timbre* of the voice, which is what gives him his peculiar charisma. One cannot say that he is in any conventional way a good singer or more than moderately accomplished as a guitarist; but since he writes the words, and feels them, before he sings them, there is an integrity about the songs, individually and taken as a body of work. The note of tragedy, the note of passion, of conviction, of scorn, in the words he sings, touch all the strings and bring out all the reverberations in the highly politicized modern Welsh culture.

'Yes, the time comes back to me' recalls, verse by verse, various key happenings in the Welsh national movement from the burning of the bombing-school at Penyberth onwards. Each verse begins with the words 'Do you remember. . .' and introduces a new incident—the drowning of the valley of Tryweryn, the election of Gwynfor Evans at Carmarthen. And it is a song that can be added to, and *has* been added to (for example when D.J.Williams died). A song such as this is a kind of popular political history for people who otherwise get little Welsh history.

'The School Song' could be called social history; it shows the anglicization of the schoolboy through the education system. Each morning his mother calls him down to breakfast in Welsh, and it is in Welsh that his parents say good-bye. Welsh is the language Christ speaks when they read the Bible in Sunday School, Welsh is the language he and his first girl-friend speak when they meet in the woods, but at school every day he gets history lessons, geography lessons, English lessons (the English words are used for these subjects, because, of course, they are taught in English) and the occasional Welsh lesson (called 'Welsh'—the English word—on the timetable) because he is a little Welshman. The whole thing goes ironically into the mode of those songs which recall an innocent childhood.

There is very little in life in Wales which does not have political overtones, which is the kind of situation in which the satirical song-writer thrives. Some of Dafydd Iwan's best songs are political in a more oblique way. 'Leave me alone' satirizes those who want to go on with their comfortable lives and keep out of politics. 'The Big Shot' (on the other side of the *Carlo* record, and a far better song) tears into the kind of provincial boss who exists in many parts of Wales, thriving on nepotism and political patronage, and tremendously taken with his own importance:

> I've been on the education committee since 1933, I know every headmaster in the county, or rather, they know me.

To attack the provincial establishment in present-day Wales, is of course, to be political. Even a Welsh rendering of 'This Land is Your Land' becomes political when people from North and South are only beginning to be conscious of themselves as one nation.

It would be wrong to suggest that all Dafydd Iwan's songs are political—he sings folk songs and love songs, children's songs and settings of Welsh poems—or indeed that all his political songs are successful; nor is he the only writer of good political and satirical songs (there are Huw Jones and Mike Stevens). But one can say of the whole Welsh pop movement that it has derived its special character, and reached its highest point, in the political songs, and also that these are the songs which, generally speaking, have sold best. Through the popular song, through Dafydd Iwan in particular, the ideas of the Welsh leadership have been able to get through, in one of the few ways now open, to the ordinary Welsh-speaker, especially in the younger generation. A sure sign that they *are* getting through is the fact that Welsh members of parliament have from time to time spoken of the pop movement as if it were a sinister conspiracy. There have been efforts to divert the pop impulse into non-political channels, too. In Investiture year a 'Song for Wales' competition was organized on television, where clearly a non-protesting approach was required. The results were lamentable as one would expect. The fact is that the liveliness of the young Welsh generation and of its singing is inseparable from the protest.

The pop movement is important beyond the songs themselves. It brings a new gaiety and lightness of touch into the Welsh movements. If you look at photographs of Saunders Lewis and Gwenallt and Kate Roberts, you see deep, suffering faces, and these perhaps can stand for the older kind of nationalist, someone deeply committed and sustained by an inner vision, but under strain. If you are going to have to live a life of protest for the foreseeable future, it is important to be able to see it as a superior way of life, a happier, more honest and more glamorous way. In its combination of hunger strikes and prison sentences with pop concerts and the irreverence of *Tafod y Ddraig*, its monthly magazine (the liveliest produced in Welsh), the Welsh Language Society both keeps in touch with the tradition of sacrifice in the older generation and moves with the informal, non-authoritarian life-style of the world's spontaneous youth movements generally. In its magazine and posters it has also come nearest to producing an indigenous style of design.

Like C.N.D. it has dissipated its energies. A lot of people in Wales thought it was a mistake for the Society to turn away from language protests to oppose the Investiture. But again like C.N.D. it would not have been itself if it had not done so. Its strength is its spontaneity and internal democracy. This produces a weakness of organization at times, and errors of judgement; but these are almost attractive vices in a world full of bureaucratized movements.

Is the Welsh Language Society a political movement? In the obvious sense, no. It does not aim at political power, either through the constitution or in any other way. It is concerned with the future of the Welsh language whether within the United Kingdom or an independent Wales. Its members will normally vote and work for *Plaid Cymru* as the party which seems to give the best chance for the future of the language, but this does not make the party and the Welsh Language Society identical, any more than C.N.D. was identical with the Labour Party.

But in another sense the movement *is* political; it is political if Saunders Lewis's interpretation of Welsh politics and history is correct. If it *is* a revolutionary act to insist on using Welsh in dealings with authority; if the introduction of Welsh signs and documents is going to strengthen the national consciousness, help to restore to Welsh people their self-respect, then a society that campaigns for these things is helping in the awakening of the Welsh people, and can only be seen as political.

But a theory needs not only to be plausible in itself; it needs to be confirmed or disproved by the way things are. The present treatment of the Welsh language by the British Government can be interpreted in two ways, each of which leads to a political conclusion for a Welsh-speaker. Either the dominant official attitude is unconcern, in which case one must work for a Welsh Government that would have greater concern; or else politicians fear the Welsh language as a political threat, in which case the opposition too is accepting Saunders Lewis's formulation.

10 / The Welsh and the Anglo-Welsh

THE RELATIONSHIP between Welsh-speakers and English-speakers in Wales is psychologically fascinating and politically crucial; it is largely unexplored, or perhaps one should say, unrevealed. It offers questions and hypotheses, but few certain answers.

The first thing that strikes one when one looks below the surface is the fluidity of the linguistic boundary here—both the geographical boundary and the line between individuals. In the older generations there are countless Welsh people who have slipped out of the language but keep a residual knowledge which they are able to use to reacquire the language if they come back to work in Welsh-speaking Wales, or retire here. In the younger generations there are smaller numbers of people who have taught themselves Welsh, sometimes to a very high level. The Welsh Theatre Company has actors who have done this, there are university lecturers in Welsh who have done it, and as the writer Bobi Jones, himself one who has learnt the language, points out: 'During each of the last three centuries there has been at least one poet in Wales creating in his second language who must be accounted among the two or three greatest poets of his age, namely Iolo Morgannwg, Islwyn and Waldo Williams'.

As you drive east out of Carmarthenshire or south down the valleys to Cardiff, the atmosphere changes, but where exactly the change occurs, and how total that change is, is very hard to decide. Swansea, where it is difficult to find Welsh displayed publicly, in fact has over 25,000 Welsh-speakers, just under one-sixth of the total. Cardiff, to which the national institutions have drawn large numbers of civil servants and professional people, has an active social and intellectual life in Welsh along-side the larger civic life in English. In rural Welsh-speaking Wales, the situation is quite different. The English-speakers have often come from England, and the two language communities live more separately.

The second thing that strikes one is how articulate and culturally active the Welsh-speaking community is compared with the much larger community of English-speakers. The former has writers and academics who in different ways and in different disciplines focus their attention on the unit of Wales. There are weekly, monthly and quarterly publications which, though sometimes amateur, are rarely trivial in their treatment of Welsh affairs. There is book production of some 150 titles per year, and many of these books, besides being in Welsh, deal with Wales in one way or another. Selective emigration, the export of talent to England, affects most spheres of life, but there are a number of institutions which help to keep some of the most talented Welsh-speakers at home. The Welsh departments of the university colleges are the places where a scholar in Welsh must make his name and his career. Aberystwyth is the college where Gwenallt lectured, Bangor the college where Sir John Morris-Jones and Williams-Parry taught and wrote. The English-speaking Welsh, unless they have access in some way to the Welsh culture, cannot feel the same about these places. The most intelligent will go elsewhere, and the University of Wales in most of its departments takes its chance, like other British universities, on the talents which the career ladder brings to its colleges at a particular stage.

All in all, Welsh-speaking Wales, despite the wedge

driven between educated and ordinary people by the mass-media in English, is a cohesive and well-articulated community; it achieves ways of looking at itself, and modifies these by a process of continuous discussion in which the best minds that identify themselves with Wales take part. It is a community of active political, religious and cultural movements. Because of all this it is possible to form a fairly clear idea of what people are experiencing and how they are reacting to that experience.

But when we come to English-speaking Wales, the same is not true to anything like the same extent. There is a provincial press, as there might be anywhere in England, following in the footsteps of metropolitan fashion but well behind. If the English-speaking Welsh find serious discussion of their problems, ways of looking at themselves, expression of their aspirations, then they must find these in the press, the institutions, the literature of the centre. But do they? They will find very little about Wales, as one would expect. This forces us back on another question, which is the fundamental one: how far do they feel themselves to be Welsh at all?

The difficulty about answering this question arises not from conflicting evidence but from the virtual absence of it. As you drive along the motorway above Port Talbot and look down on the British Steel Corporation's giant works and the town straggling at one end of it, you are brought up against the mystery of the new, relatively affluent working class of Western Europe, living what seems to be a life of passive alienation. Here thousands of people work and live with their families under the shadow of one of the biggest production units in Europe. From the point of view of the economist it might be in the Ruhr or north-eastern France: the production charts, the models of future world demand, the pricing policies on which the future of these and many other people depend, will be similar; the welfare arrangements, the pay levels, the quality and styling of the goods in the shops and the cars on the roads, these things too are becoming more alike.

But the lives that go on in the shadow of the giant machine, surely these are not wholly accounted for by the external and impersonal definitions? Sometimes in South Wales when production is paralysed by a strike, the reporters and the camera teams come down, and in addition to the details of the industrial dispute we are given a quick superficial documentary: the working-men's clubs, the new affluence, shopping in the high-street supermarkets, holidays in Majorca, set in contrast to the singing of hymns in pubs and emptying chapels, the bitter memories of the 'thirties visible in the expression of some older faces, and now perhaps shown as holding up proper integration with the modern industrial system. But soon the camera teams go, the reality of the place reverts to its unstructured, undiscussed state.

Yet one must believe, and indeed all those whose families run across educational and class boundaries know, that each of the people placed in the simple surface categories of sociology has a complexity of background and aspiration which is theirs alone. I do not mean this as a poetic statement about the uniqueness of the individual's experience, or a religious claim for the soul. It is merely that everybody is caught in a different complex of family and historical and geographical circumstances. We are linked with all sorts of different groups at different levels; to define us in terms of our packaged outward life-style and our economic interest as wage-earners is to deny our potentiality for change in other modes. One fact about the English-speaking population of South Wales is that a high percentage had Welsh-speaking parents, or at least one parent, and that many more had Welsh-speaking grandparents. Another fact is that this was a part of Britain where the Independent Labour Party was strong, where a kind of socialism had an appeal which was rather different from the sort of socialism we have in Britain now. Indeed, it is interesting that several of the early members of *Plaid Cymru* had worked hard previously for the I.L.P.

But who knows what weight to give these facts? Who can say finally that the feeling of being Welsh is played out in these parts of South Wales, or the feeling of being Socialist, despite the dead hand of the Labour establishment? Are 14,000 votes for *Plaid Cymru*, in an industrial area as far east as Caerffili, evidence of a national awakening or a by-election protest against the ruling party? Are the sources of political nationalism wholly economic in English-speaking Wales and therefore only partly the same as in the Welsh-speaking community? Are the first Welsh nursery classes in Monmouthshire, the Welsh secondary schools in Glamorganshire to which many English-speaking parents send their children, the signs of a movement back into the language or are they largely a defensive effort, a consolidation in the face of immense pressures?

These are questions that are at present answered according to people's faith rather than on any evidence. I do not think any clear answer will emerge in the short term, and things will not be settled either way in one, or two, general elections. If there *is* a movement, then it is a movement involving the drift of a generation. Nor am I sure that the awakening of people need take a particular form. The future here is not made by what happens in Wales alone. A more participant and egalitarian Britain might offer the conditions in which South Wales workers could emerge from their alienation, just as they might in a Wales that had taken responsibility for its own future. But I do believe that in whatever way our machine culture is eventually humanized, it will not be one hippie-like identity that emerges, but numbers of partially distinct cultures drawing on their own traditions. Local and international cultures will come to replace national and provincial ones.

For the moment no one can be sure what will come out of English-speaking Wales, how far it will go to meet the other culture in Welsh. All one can say is that at present the Welsh culture offers itself as a pole of humanity to the English-speaking Welsh who look into it, a world where they will be appreciated as persons and for what they can bring to that culture, whereas the English culture is mixed up with the structures of power which alienate them.

One thing needs to be made clear. No one who today speaks Welsh, gives up English and the access it offers to the wide world. The two languages serve to attach one where one belongs and to let one communicate with England and the world beyond.

Although it is hard to establish what the English-speaking Welsh are thinking and feeling, it is not wholly impossible to do so. There have been a number of Welsh authors who have written in English about Wales not as a picturesque phenomenon for the admiration of an English audience, but seriously and to try to make sense of their lives and those of their people.

One of these was the poet Idris Davies who died in 1953. The life and work of this minor poet of great integrity help, I believe, to illuminate the psychology of English-speaking Wales. Idris Davies's father was Welsh-speaking (the family had come from Cardiganshire) but the son gradually lost the language:

> I lost my native language
> For the one the Saxon spake
> By going to school by order
> For education's sake

As this rather stilted sub-Housman suggests, it was an education in English literature as well as in the English language. From school he went to Nottingham University, and then became, like many Welsh people, a teacher, trying constantly to get back to Wales to work, and for a long time failing to do so.

Idris Davies grew up with the Depression in Cwm Rhymni, and although his books were published in the late 'thirties and 'forties, they refer mainly to the 'twenties and 'thirties, the time of the general strike and mass unemployment:

> 'Ay, Ay, we remember 1926' said Dai and Shinkin,
>   As they stood on the kerb in Charing Cross
>   Road,
> 'And we shall remember 1926 until our blood is
>   dry'.

But inextricable from the theme of suffering and resistance to capitalist exploitation is the theme of Wales. It is not a fortunate theme in Idris Davies's poetry, for almost always it introduces an awkward note. It is not that we question the sincerity but rather that the expression of it makes us wince:

> And Dai's forefathers roused by song and banner,
> Alive to the passionate lore of Gwalia,
> Crowding and flocking and roaring to battle
> Between the hills and forests and the Severn
>   Sea,
> Martyrs to freedom and the Celtic dream.
> And will that dream disturb one sleeping youth
> Beneath the roofs, among the streets of Tonypandy?
> And shall the future mock our simple, simple
>   faith
> In the Progress that has scorned the native culture,
> The legend and the vision and the dream
> And a people that has nigh lost its history and
>   language
> To serve with blood and flesh the maw of Mammon.

The first point which this extract illustrates is the way

the oppression of human beings in South Wales, as with Kate Roberts' quarrymen in the North, is not easily separated from the pressures on them *as Welsh people*, which robbed them of their language and their history. But the passage also shows, at the level of style, how difficult it was for Idris Davies to write in English about his country and his feelings for it. All that he can command is the vocabulary of the romanticizing nineteenth century in England, with all it archaism and vagueness: *lore, Gwalia, Celtic dream, nigh lost*. How far this is from what we find in modern Welsh literature. And in the reference to 'the native culture' we see what happens when the insider is forced to use the language of the outsider for his deepest feelings.

Alternating with the high style is the colloquial, pathetic, regional style. Here is a grocer in a South Wales town speaking in one of the poems:

'Mrs. Evans, fach, you want butter again.
How will you pay for it now, little woman
With your husband out on strike, and full
Of the fiery language?'

Lines such as these can be moving if you give all your sympathy to the situation, withhold your irony. But most readers are going to be deflected from the proper effect by the feeling that the language is picturesque or even pathetically comic. The difference between Gwenallt and Idris Davies writing about the Depression is the difference between tragedy and pathos. This is not due wholly to a difference of talent. Time and place, and the relation of the language used to the place described, *do* exert a force, impose limitations. I have probably given the impression that Idris Davies is a much worse poet than he actually is. When he can isolate the theme of the exploited and suffering miner from the specifically Welsh context, his writing can be powerful:

O what is man that coal should be so careless of

him
And what is coal that there should be so much blood
  upon it?

But he cannot sustain this because he is trying to convey
the life of the whole South Wales community in the Depression, and when he comes up against its Welshness he is
left without words and styles. Gwenallt had words and
references heavy with the experience of the centuries,
the dignity of the terms in which successive generations
of the same people have suffered. English cannot provide the same for Idris Davies, for the people he writes
about were not really English, had not used that
language for centuries. So he has to make the styles he
has come across in English literature fit his emotions as
best they can. In the obvious gap between his style and
his intention lies his painful sincerity. And sometimes
one catches through it a glimpse of the old Welsh
tradition:

Let's go to Barry Island, Maggie fach,
And give all the children a day by the sea,
And sherbet and buns and paper hats
And a rattling ride on the Figure Eight;
We'll have tea on the sands and rides on the
  donkeys,
And sit in the evening with the folk of Cwm
  Rhondda,
Singing the sweet hymns of Pantycelyn
When the sun goes down behind the rock islands.

There is a brave defeatedness about Idris Davies's people, as there is in his cadences, and in this singing of
Pantycelyn's hymns one senses an obscure instinct for
consolation holding on to the Welsh past.

It seems to me that industrial South Wales has suffered a double wound—the sheer hardship of industrial
life with the humiliation of the years of unemployment;
and added to this the loss of the language and all that it
contained in the way of spiritual resources with which to

meet that suffering. There is a humiliation in losing your language as there is in the indignity of the means test, and though it may seem a secondary kind of humiliation, it can leave a mark that lasts a long time. In any case, the two humiliations are mixed up with one another and are commemorated in what is one of Idris Davies's finest poems:

> I saw the ghosts of The Successful Century
> Marching on the ridges of the sunset
> And wandering among derelict furnaces,
> And they had not forgotten their humiliation,
> For their mouths were full of curses.
> And I cried aloud, O what shall I do for my
> fathers
> And the land of my fathers?
> But they cursed and cursed and would not answer
> For they could not forget their humiliation.

In his book of essays on Anglo-Welsh authors, *The Dragon has Two Tongues*, Glyn Jones relates how after returning to Wales, Idris Davies taught himself Welsh again, even writing one or two poems in the language:

> In common, perhaps, with most Welsh-speaking Welshmen, his attitude upon many issues came gradually very near to that of the Welsh Nationalists. I do not think his conversion was sudden, or that in looking at questions from a specifically Welsh angle he abandoned his deeply rooted Socialism, that Socialism of brotherhood rather than elect-rification.

When the volume of Idris Davies's *Selected Poems*, chosen by T.S. Eliot at Faber, came out a fortnight before the Welsh poet's death, the last poem in the book, with the same sincerity showing through the same stilted grand style, was a tribute to Saunders Lewis and his action in burning down the bombing-school at Penyberth.

Many, perhaps most Anglo-Welsh writers, are by today much more explicitly nationalist than Idris Davies ever was. One reason for this may be that they are not now pulled in different ways by their feeling for their own country and the ideals of world socialism. The more attractive forms of socialist thought are now those which speak of participation and control, by those who belong to each other in their place of work or through a shared culture.

The change in the tone of modern Anglo-Welsh writing is explained in this way by Glyn Jones:

> It must be increasingly difficult, I feel, for any novelist to write well about Wales, if he doesn't know something of the history and language of the country. Wales was plundered in the 'thirties of her picturesque features; there is no longer novelty or quaintness in portrayals of her superficial differences from England, and her grotesque cranks, oddities and eccentrics have long been creamed off for the exuberant and colourful pages of Dylan Thomas, Rhys Davies, Gwyn Jones and Caradoc Evans. A younger generation to which Emyr Humphreys belongs, is forced to look deeper into Welsh society if it is dissatisfied with a mere repetition of established patterns.

And not only novelists. In the recent poetry of R.S.Thomas one catches the note of desperation and resistance that is hardly to be distinguished from a great deal of what is being written in Welsh. The same could be said of half a dozen lesser-known poets whose work can be seen regularly in *Poetry Wales*.

Glyn Jones points out that many of the best-known Anglo-Welsh writers (and they include Glyn Jones himself) are also able to speak Welsh. English became the language of their writing only because it was the language of their education. This, of course, makes them less than wholly representative of the English-speaking population of Wales. But one should note that there are other writers, having no recent family connection with Welsh, who have made the effort to learn it, or have found out enough about the culture to bring them to a very similar position. The truth seems to be that people can feel deprived of their language even if they can remember nothing of it in the history of their families. All that is needed is some sense of identification with Wales for the sensitive person to be led back to investigate his or her roots. When that happens, they find something which, apart from belonging to them, is attractive by its qualities of depth and humanity, and by its history of struggle.

What seems to be happening in the literary sphere is that the middle ground is disappearing. Those writers in English who regard themselves as Welsh are being drawn closer to the Welsh culture, but there are no doubt plenty of English writers, born in Wales, who have never turned their faces back in its direction. They are probably not known to one as Welsh writers. In between these poles, the regional school of writing, the English book with a Welsh flavour, seems to be dying out.

But how far is a movement in literature a guide to what is happening in society? I doubt whether Anglo-Welsh writers exert much influence in Wales. An Anglo-Welsh poet published here will be lucky if his or her books sell in a quarter of the numbers which a Welsh poet can expect to sell, although the potential audience of the former is nearly four times as large. This reflects the lack of psychological and institutional cohesion in the English-speaking community in Wales.

But do Anglo-Welsh writers express what is to be found deep down in many more Welsh people? Clearly, this movement to uncover your nation's past through a language, through the study of history and literature, is something for which the educated people are better equipped, and for which they usually have more time. But that it can draw in a quite different sort of person is shown by the case of David John Underhill, a young lorry-driver from Bridgend in Glamorganshire, one of those accused, but acquitted, in the Free Wales Army Trial of 1969. On his release from prison he was interviewed at some length by the Welsh weekly *Y Cymro*. He said:

> It is difficult for you who are born Welsh-speakers to understand how much the language can mean to us who are born without it. The Bridgend area in which I was brought up lost its Welsh entirely. The first time that I came into contact with the language on any large scale was three years ago at the National Eisteddfod in Aberafan (Port Talbot). I happened to ask someone to translate a Welsh sentence that I found in a book. It read: "A nation that loses its language loses its heart" and it was these words that started my interest in the language.

> 'I began to ask myself why no Welsh was spoken in my area. I came to know about the Act of Union and its purpose of wiping the Welsh language off the face of the earth; and about the "Welsh Not" policy in the schools. This was why the language had died out in Bridgend. I promised myself I would learn the language, and I joined an evening class. By today I can speak Welsh fairly fluently. . .

But at any time the number of English-speakers who are orientated to the Welsh language is bound to be small. Whereas Welsh-speakers live in a culture which constantly directs their attention to the language, English-speakers live in the culture we all know, which seems to encourage multiple cultural interests but takes seriously only questions of production and consumption and the control of these processes. If the feelings made explicit in Anglo-Welsh poetry, or which became a personal commitment in the case of David John Underhill, exist for the majority of English-speaking Welsh people, then they are well to the back of the mind. But the way the language is successfully played on in the politics of Wales suggests that there *are* feelings there, even a communal guilt, while such statistics as we have indicate a considerable piety towards Welsh. Thus a survey, the results of which were published in the *Western Mail* at the end of 1968, showed 50 percent as wanting more Welsh taught in the schools; 52 per cent thinking that every sign and form throughout Wales should be bilingual, and almost everyone thinking that these should be bilingual in Welsh-speaking areas.

The English-speaking and Welsh-speaking Welsh are not two quite separate language groups who happen to be rubbing shoulders, like English and French-speakers in Quebec Province; they are one group which has suffered a split in its consciousness, and this produces a curious emotional ambivalence which can be exploited for conflict but which is also the hope for cultural and political solidarity.

As the educated Welsh-speakers look at the new affluent working-class of South Wales they are bound to see people who have lost a culture and gained only a higher standard of living, people made particularly vulnerable to commercially fostered pseudo-values by their own rootlessness, people who have lost the dignity of a language and acquired a despised and comic dialect of English. As the description of social process this is not so far from the mark, but when applied to individuals, whose language is for them an accident, it is condescending and offensive. Great individual achievement can be built from a shattered cultural background as well as inside a cohesive culture. The case of Dylan Thomas shows this.

It may seem that I have been saying that Welsh people write better in Welsh, or that they can only write truly about Wales in Welsh. Things are more complicated than that. A writer does not often choose a language; it chooses him and is the result of a series of accidents. As Glyn Jones has suggested, it is not which is the *first* language that is all-important, but which language captures the adolescent's imagination when he or she first discovers literature. There are, of course, particular dangers when you come to write about your country in a language which is new to it and which carries the weight of another culture. We have seen how this created difficulties for Idris Davies. But one must believe that a style *can* be found that both does justice to the Welsh reality and communicates adequately with English readers. This book is itself based on the assumption that such a style can be found. R.S.Thomas's more recent poems are a triumph in this respect. In them the note of desperation and of protest rings true as a style in English, and it is true to the Welsh language culture in which he lives his life.

To sum up, one needs, whether discussing writers or people in general, to be able to separate patterns of cultural prosperity and decadence and disintegration— which undoubtedly exist and put certain limitations on the individual—from that individual's innate capacity to find a way out. In Wales this distinction is not always made, and English-speakers sometimes detect and resent a sense of superiority in the Welsh-speaker.

But fortunately there is another element, increasingly present in the Welsh-speaker's attitude, which overcomes any condescension: this is the consciousness that any future Wales and the Welsh language may have, must depend very largely on the English-speakers in Wales.

There is only one *real* (as opposed to psychological) element which causes friction between the two languages under the present administrative arrangements. A number of jobs, particularly at the higher levels of employment, are advertised with a Welsh language qualification. This excludes a majority of the otherwise qualified applicants, whereas if no such qualification is required, the Welsh-speaker (who also knows English) still has an equal change. Thus in 1970 the BBC in Cardiff required a

117

head of news and current affairs. To have appointed a person who did not speak Welsh, and therefore could not keep up with the Welsh press and with all that was happening in Welsh, would have been disastrous; but at the same time the introduction of the language requirement undoubtedly excluded some otherwise well-qualified applicants.

The introduction of bilingualism in Wales as a deliberate policy would be felt by many people as a threat to their jobs. If Welsh-speakers are to have the right, as a matter of course and not by special application, to do their business with government departments and public corporations in Welsh, then these departments will have to employ more Welsh-speakers, who will acquire in this way a monopoly of many of the best jobs going.

At present there is no way of doing justice to both language groups. What is needed is to codify the situation, so that people know where they stand, what guarantees they have so far as their jobs are concerned; and at the same time the administrative structure needs to be reorganized so that, where possible, parallel Welsh and English departments offer security and promotion to the top. Sometimes a territorial distinction might have to be made, with English and Welsh speakers enjoying majority rights in certain areas, minority rights in others. Welsh-speakers have no interest in getting a phoney official bilingualism everywhere, but they do need to be able to reorganize the administrative structure. Of course this is expensive and disruptive, and a country such as Belgium has done it because in the end it is less expensive and less disruptive than a language-conflict. But how do you bring about change in the bureaucracy? Does one always have to have trouble first?

In Wales now we are faced with more than bureaucratic immobility. There is actual exploitation in the English-language press here and in the speeches of some M.P.s, of the employment fears at the back of English-speakers' minds. Campaigns for linguistic equality are described as 'fanatical', and the people behind the campaigns are accused of trying to 'impose' their views on the majority. But what English-speaker is threatened by a bilingual sign? And in what conceivable Welsh state of the future could less than one fifth of the population force its views on the remainder?

It is true that some nationalists dream of a great swing back to the language. If one admits the possibility that there will be a political swing to nationalism after centuries of rule from England, then one must also admit the possibility that we shall have a situation in which hundreds of thousands of people are going to will that their children grow up speaking Welsh. But this cannot be called likely.

The Welsh-language community, living in an atmosphere of crisis, thinks easily in these revolutionary terms, but English-speaking Wales is in a different situation. It is a province slowly coming back to life and looking for something to replace the second-rate greyness of its life. If enough people attach themselves to the notion of Wales, if enough talent stays in the country and devotes itself to building a better society here, then changes will come. The people who make such a movement, whatever their first language, are bound to look for support to the Welsh language culture which conserves the Welsh tradition unbroken. But regardless of any question of sentiment, it is clear that left to themselves Welsh-speakers and English-speakers would have to work things out on a realistic and amicable basis. Each language group is large enough, within Wales, to demand that the other respect its rights. But we do not have the institutions within which to work things out, and so from time to time we project our fears and frustrations on to the other language group. The interest of all the nationalist and language movements is to conciliate the two groups, to bring them to feel their common background and interdependence. The interest of the British parties, and particularly the Labour Party in Wales, sadly for everyone, seems to lie in exploiting fears.

11 / 'The Sound of the Wind that's Blowing'

ANYONE WHO has read this far will feel that they have been taken through a labyrinth of frustrations, a world where the sense of accumulated grievance has eaten deep into the psychology of a whole group. There *is* a wound, and this is the source of so many things: the lack of self-confidence both in individuals and in the social group, but also of the great introspective literature in Welsh, and of the continuing live religious tradition. In the knowledge of ourselves as a suppressed group there is also a kind of historical knowledge which is denied to more fortunate peoples. It telescopes the past, making it possible for Welsh people to look at the thirteenth century and the days of Welsh independence, rather as Balkan peoples looked across the centuries to the time before Turkish occupation. This is one of the most difficult things for the English to understand: and it must seem as if only a fevered romantic imagination would want to bring to life tapestry figures such as Llywelyn the Great or Owain Glyndŵr. Yet both these names can appear in the popular songs of Dafydd Iwan.

There is another, more Marxist sense, in which the suppressed group carries within it the sense of history; it cannot but feel the pressure of historical movement, historical direction. While the comfortable, adjusted social group can live in the present, we have to live in the past and in the future for the consciousness of suppression has implicit in it the notion of liberation and emergence.

Therefore this same wound is also the source of the political protest that has led us, in this century and the last, to support whichever was the radical movement of the time, in the hope that it might bring us, too, out into the light.

It is worth here noting our ready identification with subject peoples everywhere. One of the best-selling Welsh books of 1969 was T.J.Davies's biography of Martin Luther King. It is a popular biography rather than a work of original research, but the writing has the kind of edge and urgency to it that only comes when a subject touches an author's own exposed nerves. An indirect comparison with Wales runs throughout the book, and sometimes it becomes direct and explicit. Just as many older black people had been told they were inferior until they had come to believe it, so Welsh people had been conditioned to accept the offical deprecatory estimate of their own language and culture:

> Most important was the new spirit among the Blacks. They were a people that had been trampled on, that had had every ounce of pride, self-confidence and self-respect squeezed out of them. They were servile, the children of oppression. A Welshman can understand and appreciate these things. His heart responds to the heartbeat of the children of oppression, and he knows what centuries of being held down can mean to a people's spirit.

Like American Blacks, the Welsh have identified themselves with the Jewish people. In both cases this stems from a Protestant, Biblical culture. But while that explains what made the identification *possible*, the depth of feeling comes from the common experience of exiled or rejected groups. Listening to our hymn-singing, who can doubt that like that of the American Black it expresses the yearning of a group whose identity has been suppressed, and the same internal triumph over external circumstance.

The identification with the Jews was carried to its furthest and most explicit in a short note written by Saunders Lewis in *Radio Times* in February 1970, when his play *Esther* was given a magnificent television performance. After explaining that it was Racine's *Esther* rather than the Old Testament story that moved him to write on this subject in the first place, he added:

> Between my time and Racine's there lay Hitler's attempt in Germany, Poland and Austria, to destroy the Jewish nation utterly. Between us lay the camps and the gas chambers and the bodies of men and women and children piled high on each other. And I could not forget that my own nation too was being wiped out, just as efficiently, though not in such obviously diabolical ways.

There is, of course, all the difference in the world between physical annihilation and cultural annihilation, which is what makes Saunders Lewis's formulation appear so extreme. But it is a formulation to which a Welsh person can respond.

Yet hardly any of us lives in the Welsh culture alone. Although up to a point alienated from the English culture, we profit by it to reach out for ideas to a wider world (it is probably this free movement of ideas into Welsh through bilingualism that has kept the culture as contemporary as it is). What we represent therefore, is not a ghetto consciousness but a torn consciousness, something which it is easier for a Yoruba writing in English, or a West Indian of Indian extraction, or a Spanish or French Basque to understand than it is for an English person. It might be easier for us all if the Welsh language and all it embodies had long ago been wiped out. There would not be this torn state. Most thinking Welsh people must at some time have wanted to get away from the eternal and obsessive problem of the future of the language, the future of their own identity, but it is not something one can relinquish by taking thought. One can, of course, *deny* one's Welshness, and numbers of Welsh people have done this, particularly in the older generation, at great psychological cost to themselves. The alternative is to live out the tension, to try to work it out by changing the situation. The notion of ambivalence seems to me crucial for the understanding of Wales from outside; and for us within, the bringing of the ambivalence into consciousness is a necessary step towards working it out.

The worlds of the English and Welsh languages, although they occupy the same geographical territory, are as distinct as those of some major European languages, because they represent a specialization of function. English is pre-eminently analytic, operational, the language of power and manipulation; technical language and advertising have not wholly driven out the language of poetry, human feeling and passion, but are certainly driving them into a corner. Welsh has specialized as the language of small human communities, of domestic life, of religion, of certain traditional occupations such as farming, and of literature. It is not the language of power, and neither, therefore, of responsibility.

One task the Welsh-speaker faces in trying to overcome the tension of this split identity is that of assuming responsibility, with some of the moral corruption which that involves. In a very striking English poem, Glyn Jones imagines the mixed beauty and horror of a Welsh state in which the flag with the red dragon waves over all:

> The Red Dragon flies forward; every dewdrop is a peacock.
> The great sun floats awash in the bay. Only Welsh is exchanged
> On Sunday beaches hideous with shit and transistors.

The Red Dragon triumphs over the silver-backed

smokes.
Until the city is a cairn, the language of Llanrhaeadr
and Pantycelyn
Shall be used for the utterance of her cruelty, her
banalities, her lies.

The Red Dragon droops over the inherited gaol.

This is the kind of doubt one is bound to have about all political action, but at the same time the kind of doubt that has to be overcome if one is ever to make the world better. Like Spanish anarchist villagers we have got so used to equating power with evil and centralism, that we find it hard to move from eloquent protest at the injustice of things to the taking of responsibility for the future. Our acquaintance with power, with advancement, has been usually through England and almost always through English. Our Welsh life has been an inward one.

The pull of these different poles accounts for a great deal in our public life. Fervent nationalists turn into Labour M.P.s overnight in a mixture of careerism with the belief that you can do more for your country if you have some access to real power. Very often the Welsh who go furthest in public life are those whose real political position is uncertain. A 'good' appointment in Wales (and it can be paralleled in satrapies such as Georgia or Catalonia) is one that selects someone who has certain characteristics of the 'good' Welshman—a real command of the language, and attachment to the cultural institutions—but who at the same time is careful or timid enough not to worry the appointing authorities, who are usually English. Nor is it easy to make proper judgements on such people. Have they done all that can be done for Wales within the existing power-structure? Or are they a subtle part of the machine which represses the Welsh language?

Another interesting phenomenon of Welsh life which

confirms the analysis of ambivalence, and shows its interaction with the job structure, is the life pattern of many public figures; a student career of fairly passionate nationalism gives way to a careful public career, but on retirement the passionate nationalist again emerges.

The process of gaining courage, taking responsibility for ourselves, brings us inevitably into a position of protest and resistance. One is saying that British society too must change, so as to allow the expression of our Welshness in outward forms. It must itself become more human.

There is a different complex of values embodied in every language; languages have different 'intentions' (to use Walter Benjamin's term) and full translation becomes possible only when those intentions become the same. It is easier to imagine Kate Roberts or Saunders Lewis well-translated into Russian than it is into English: the note of depth, of suffering, of moral purity goes less easily into the ironic mode of modern English. A purposeful, revolutionary Britain, or Europe, would take it for granted that a separate language-group should have greater autonomy, and thus make it less necessary for the Welsh to assert their difference. There would be no gap between the moral aspiration inside the Welsh community and the morality proclaimed by the larger unit. Notions of virtue, the setting of high aims, the dream of a just form of human organization—these *are* factors in politics, after all, and they *can* override national differences. But they can also co-operate with national aims, as they now do in Wales, since there is no sign of a democratic breakthrough on the British or Western European scale.

What we need is space to manoeuvre institutionally, constitutionally, space in which the psychological ambivalence can be worked out, in which the internal identity can find itself in new external and institutional forms. If one looks at the map of Western Europe, one sees that this is not a problem peculiar to us. There are the Basques and the Bretons and the Catalans and the Friesians and the Alsatians, all representing a different complex of historical experience, a different linguistic situation. Perhaps there is no future for the dream of the small nation-state; but the only person who has the right to tell us this is someone who also wants to see the end of the large nation-state.

At present we in Wales are unable to establish any kind of identity. We are not a part of England and yet we are not a country on our own. Economically we can clearly never be independent of England entirely, yet the present degree of dependence leaves us wholly without protection. Those of us who are Welsh-speaking cannot establish a proper relationship between the languages. If Welsh was secure and officially supported, the normal language of our everyday lives in certain parts of Wales, English would be our international language and the two languages would not be in competition. Welsh people who do not speak the language still feel the ambivalence; 'Despite our speech we are not English' (R.S.Thomas). Worst of all, the lines of communication which run to London offer no way of working out the relationship between Welsh and English-speakers.

Shall we ever get the space, the opportunity to turn to each other and work these things out? In terms of British politics, Welsh-speakers are very poorly placed. As a minority within Wales they must lean on the problematical support of English-speaking Welsh people whose own political direction is uncertain. We are also spread out unevenly over the country. Nowhere is there a wholly Welsh community, except perhaps at the level of the smallest village. There is no town that is wholly Welsh, and towns are traditionally the centres of political organization. Even as a pressure group, Welsh-speakers lack power in places where it is really useful—for example in the business community and inside the English communications media. Jews in Britain present a very marked contrast in these respects.

What is more, any future that is to be made for Welsh within the conventions of British democracy, will have to be made very quickly. The movement of the English population in the next twenty years will almost certainly result in the Midlands spilling over into large areas of Wales. Without the means of self-protection which one's own government affords, it is hard to say whether overspill development or the present depopulation and lack of development present the greater threat.

While *Plaid Cymru* seems to have an electoral chance, Welsh-speakers will for the most part continue to think in terms of conventional politics. Perhaps the British democratic institutions will, after all, work for us. Perhaps we shall overcome the disadvantage of living in a state where press and television are among the most centralized in the world, and where, as a result, whatever the local issues, a fairly uniform national swing has been observable in recent general elections. Perhaps a common loyalty will be forged between English and Welsh-speaking Welsh, in which case Welsh-speakers will live in a unit small enough to give them bargaining power, under a government which if not wholly their own is well-disposed to their interest. Or perhaps we should work and wait for the kind of British Government that has the imagination, the dynamism, to do something about Wales, and to assert human priorities, the type of government that would, within a short period, set up a Welsh language television channel, an institute of higher education working through Welsh, and control population movement and industrial development with some thought for the futures of the different linguistic and cultural communities that exist in these islands.

But I cannot conceal my fear that we shall not win or be granted enough political power in Wales, at least in time to do any good. What are the alternatives, and what strengths has the Welsh-language community to draw on?

I believe that this community is capable of becoming politically radicalized, and that this is what will happen. We have the advantage of a relatively high standard of education, a still fairly untrivialized population and a reasonably well-developed political awareness. There is also the cohesiveness of the social group, the relative unimportance of money and class distinctions of the kind which make England consume itself in endless class querulousness. There is strength of will too, and among the young the disappearance of the old servility and playing safe. But on top of all this the Welsh movements will need an audacious imagination, a way of seeing society subtle enough to interpret our dilemma as Welsh people, but wide enough to set us in a world context and give us solidarity with other groups and classes of people. As English population floods into Wales we shall need more and more to provide a culture that not so much defends itself by exclusion, as absorbs people by its superior humanity.

One does not have to look far to find theories that fit our situation. Marcuse's indictment of the kind ˙of technological society that turns us into part of the machine of production and consumption makes a good starting-point:

> Not only a specific form of government or party rule makes for totalitarianism, but also a specific system of production and distribution which may well be compatible with a 'pluralism' of parties, newspapers, 'countervailing powers'.

This system has no place for Welsh at all. 650,000 people

speaking another language are merely an inconvenience, an obstacle to the rationalization of the machine, an expensive extra programme for the computer. But what *is* an 'economic' size of community? The machine presses towards the definition of community as the maximum market, unhindered in the case of Wales by the political power with which people might resist this tendency. The system wants us as consumers, but it does not want us as Welsh-speakers.

There is no real distinction to be drawn between the private and public sectors. As British citizens the state may intervene to protect us at the margins from the worst excesses of advertising, but it does not defend us as Welsh-speakers. It would be considered ridiculous to insist that advertising to Welsh-speaking areas, or a proportion of all advertising in the whole of Wales, should be in Welsh.

Meanwhile the public sector itself becomes more and more dominated by administrative rather than political decisions, that is to say, by decisions internal to the machine itself. For the bureaucracy too, Welsh-speakers are a nuisance.

Of course it is not only the Welsh who are the victims of the machine. Welsh children brainwashed by hour upon hour of English television from infancy are not more conditioned to accept the values of machine society than are English children; but if they keep their hold on Welsh at all they are more likely to become aware of the brainwashing. One of the great values of the Welsh language is that in a world where social controls are built into the individual through the pattern of work and leisure, where the mass-media offer unreal choices and controversies to the point where people's aspirations and even their protests are conditioned, it preserves an area of inner freedom, of conscious alienation from the system, and at the same time a means of contact which by-passes, indeed short-circuits the machine.

Modern technological society needs very delicate social controls over its citizens, since its own organization is very delicate and vulnerable. In present conditions, the Welsh language and the culture it embodies is likely at all times to produce unpredictable and disruptive courses of action. A campaign to establish proper bilingualism in Wales is in fact a more direct threat to bureaucracy than the passion and violence of an anti-Vietnam war demonstration in London. The latter is the kind of protest for which the system allows. If the Welsh movements were to take a more violent turn, even quite a few people could cause vast disruption in the complicated web of public services and communications within such a densely populated country as Britain. To the system, the area in which people think in Welsh is an area of chaos, a latent threat which at times turns into a physical threat. But seen from within, this Welsh world is one in which more humane criteria apply. It is part of the 'great refusal' to be absorbed into a system which seems blind. This may seem an extreme and theoretical analysis. There *is* something theoretical about all consciousness that is alienated from the world as it is. But the extremity of the analysis is something that corresponds to the mode in which the best of modern Welsh literature is written, and in which many intelligent Welsh people think when they are thinking about Wales, One can even say that there is no alternative Welsh mode of looking at the situation—only varying degrees of compromise with the system. Whereas whole classes of English people might find the Marcusian analysis wildly irrelevant, any Welsh-speaker who reads this book is bound to feel that there is some truth here for their own situation. We may not be all politically radicalized, but we are all very easily capable of becoming so.

What sort of future can we then predict? This cannot

be fully answered without making predictions about British society too. But if present trends continue, and there is no mass movement in Wales to establish a nation-state—a development I cannot think likely— Welsh-speakers will have to move urgently and in new ways to preserve their community, setting up parallel co-operative institutions of all kinds which they will run in their own way and in Welsh—shops, transport, housing and business finance, farming and, if they can find the money, small factories. This will have to start in a very small way, since there are no really large accumulations of capital within the Welsh-speaking community. One can foresee a time when all Welsh-speakers will be asked to contribute a proportion of their income to these parallel institutions, and to leave land and property to the Welsh community as a collective.

Moves of this kind would imply a great mental break with the money system and with profit-maximizing. They imply reorganizing life on a basis that puts the future of a valued human community first. And there is a continuity between these notions of intentional community and the natural communities of the past in which farms were not stretches of land to be bought and sold by people who moved on, but inheritances to be cared for and passed down. Welsh-speakers have come to the point, rather sooner than others, when it is apparent that if their community is to go on existing at all the time has come to put something back into it. People everywhere in industrialized countries have realized after two centuries of ruthlessly exploiting nature that the time has come to conserve it. But how limited the view of conservation usually is. If the people have gone, and the memories have gone, and the literature that records the interaction of people with the landscape has gone, and we come and place plastic litter sacks on the sterilized green slopes, how can we talk of conservation.

The truth is that our whole industrial civilisation has been based on exploitation—not only the exploitation of workers by owners, and of the countryside for profit, but the exploitation of everything, including ourselves, in a blind urge to produce more and more. We have looked on everything, in Marcuse's phrase 'as the stuff of domination'. We have been concerned, in Wales more than most places, with 'getting on', not realizing that this was a way of getting out of one's responsibility to the community for the total quality of life. But everywhere the air of progress has turned subtly sour and we all have to cast around for some closer, more human and intimate basis on which to reconstruct our lives. For some of us that basis is Welsh. That is the community which we must put something back into.

About a mile from where I now live in Cardiganshire James Kitchener Davies, the poet, dramatist and *Plaid Cymru* activist was born and brought up. The farmhouse has fallen in, as have some fifteen others in the immediate neighbourhood within the last fifty years (though the names are still remembered, and in some cases the names of the individual fields). In the long radio poem completed when he lay dying in 1952, *The Sound of the Wind that's Blowing,* he recalls all the fields about the house and the hedges he used to plant with his father to give shelter from the wind; also the hedges made by his grandfathers, who had planted a sweet plum-tree here and there among the thorn trees for the enjoyment of later times. (What has happened to us, that living so much more easily, we have lost this kind of care?) He goes on to develop the hedges and the wind as a metaphor. All his life he sees himself as wanting to build himself refuges, asking to be allowed the comfort of his family and friends,

> The small habits of my civilisation
> And the morals that are in fashion among my

people
and to be spared the call to saintliness. This is a very fine
personal and religious poem, which does not stop it having reverberations of a national kind.

The image of Wales as a garden, a vineyard, a
landscape shaped and humanized by the care of generations, is one that recurs in our literature. The wind too is
always there, usually with its religious meaning of something cleansing, blowing away the props of our complacency. The actual garden is fast disappearing; the
hedgerows are literally bulldozed down, the cultivated
land turns out to be marginal land for the central
economic planner. And the warm, human Welsh community within which one could snuggle away from the
centres of English power where the decisions were made
on our behalf, that too is being broken down. The truth is
brought home that although one can survive for a long
time by lying low, there comes a time when defenceless-
ness means death. We have to get up and stand in the
wind, imagine a new future. As Unamuno said (and
being a Basque he knew exactly what was at stake):
tradition should be like a skeleton, inside the body, giving it strength, not outside, like the hard shell of a crab,
holding the life in. Very soon there will be no quiet, comfortable way left of being Welsh; 'traditional' Welshness
seems more and more a sham. We either have to lie
down as if dead or do something new.

But what if the whole of this book is fine words and
theorizing that will come to nothing; what if all the
Welsh movements can do is break themselves against
the walls of bureaucratic indifference and popular
incomprehension? 'This is the botched land' writes
R.S. Thomas, and perhaps we shall go down in a splutter
of weak explosions, minor sabotage, student protest
endlessly ineffectual, since Welsh students are outnum-
bered by English even in their own university. Are we to

foresee a decade in which there will always be a handful of young people in the prisons of Wales, while the press and the mass-media keep their conscience clean by inveighing against injustice in far parts of the world? Anyone who see to it that their children grow up speaking Welsh, as I do, must think of this too. What if they were to take the language and the condition of their people seriously?

One is giving them a part in a sadness and in a struggle, the end of which cannot be foreseen; but one is also giving them access to a tradition of great moral and emotional strength. Nor is this a bad place and time to live; there is an attraction about the modern Welsh culture and its resistance to the inhumanity of the machine. The fields are greener and the sea bluer because of the unseen company of past generations. There is a kind of intensity here that flows below the slack surface of British normality, a constant pressure on the individual to contribute something to the community, to do something for it. Passion and action find their place alongside calculation and analysis, moral imperatives alongside technical expertise. The culture offers an atmosphere curiously like that of semi-developed and potentially revolutionary countries, an atmosphere with depth and density too, unlike that of the fashionable cults transplanted from China and Cuba to the flats of North London. It springs from a real situation and has a real tradition behind it. And there is still enough human warmth left in the community, and enough of the sweetness and dignity of the traditional life, to sustain one. The worst thing is to be in isolation from people of goodwill in other places, and it is to help break out of this that I have written the book.

12 / The Welsh Extremist Revisited—a Postcript in 1990

TWENTY YEARS ago I was writing the book that was to be published as *The Welsh Extremist*. I was also preparing the first number of the magazine *Planet*. I had recently returned to Wales after many years away. It was a time of commitment, you may say.

And is this, you ask, a time for reminiscence, the nostalgia or disillusion of the Welsh generation of '68? Not reminiscence for its own sake, I hope. If I go over the experience of writing 'the little red book' and having it published, it is so as to try to understand how committed books of this kind enter into social process. If Raymond Williams features large in this essay, it is because he has helped me to understand my place in that process. One needs to test one's personal experience against a set of ideas and terms that might be generally applicable. If they *are* generally applicable, then they can also be applied to the situation that has developed in Wales in the twenty years since the first publication of *The Welsh Extremist*. So this is also an essay about where we stand now.

Ever since I was a student, I can remember the to-and-fro of the same argument: on the one hand, one must engage, commit oneself, become something more than a floating individual without a purpose; on the other, one must not sell one's soul, one must avoid writing shallow rhetoric and propaganda. Orwell laid down the guidelines for this dilemma in the the Thirties: politics vs literature, and the necessity for both. He then went on to make the dilemma into a way of life and of writing about himself.

Living in other countries and reading other literatures made me increasingly doubt the terms of that liberal dilemma: African writers educating their people out of the self-contempt imposed by colonialism, or Russian dissident writers recording the life of the prisons and camps, were political not by some conscious act of allegiance, but because to render unflinchingly those things which had always been thought the province of 'art'—the texture of life, moral choices, sufferings, joys, betrayals—was perceived in their societies as political. These writers did not seem to be solving a personal dilemma or even to have much choice—their engagement with life and with writing made them a voice for others. Did they choose to write or were they in some sense chosen to express a wider social experience?

To turn back to Wales and to my own experience is to be conscious of great differences of scale and of the many ironies that surround our relatively petty oppressions and struggles. Bearing all that in mind, I nevertheless have to say that my own experience of writing a 'political' book was less a matter of conscious choice, and more a making contact with something buried in myself—and, as it turned out, with something more widely present in society. Yes, I think there was a moment when (in a phrase from one of Walcott's plays) 'my feet touch ground'. I think I was whitewashing the house while my small children played in the field, and I thought I'll stay with this struggle, not as a journalist observing it, *ond fel Cymro;* and put the novel for which I had a bursary aside and started to write *The Welsh Extremist;* but that was merely the moment in which things that had long been forming emerged into full consciousness. Equally I don't deny the existence of superficial, willed and rhetorical elements in *The Welsh Extremist*—tones of special pleading . Those, I think, are its weaknesses as propaganda. The deeper, emotional charge which various readers have remarked on, and which perhaps makes it in places more successful propaganda, came from an altogether less conscious level.

As it happens, time has allowed me to uncover one of the unconscious springs of feeling. The late and generous John Tripp on more than one occasion singled out for praise a passage which comes at the end of *The Welsh Extremist* and which contains the following sentence: 'The fields are greener and the sea bluer because of the unseen company of past generations.' Only years later did I realize that this is a translated semi-quotation from Waldo Williams's poem *'Geneth Ifanc'*, moved to a different context. I had omitted Waldo from the sections of the book that deal with twentieth-century Welsh literature because I felt unready to write about him in the way I had done of Saunders Lewis, Kate Roberts and Gwenallt. But is he there more powerfully because unconsciously? And is not something more than individual being transmitted through my writing at this point?

Most people who write must, at least once or twice, have felt that a particular piece 'writes them' rather than gets written by them. I have felt that on two other, quite different writing occasions. What was different in the case of *The Welsh Extremist* was the social confirmation of the individual experience. I have written other books, of an academic kind, which have drawn on average a half-dozen letters each over the years from friends, colleagues and students. Even my journalism, which is not always free of the unworthy aim of stirring things up, rarely attracts more than one or two outraged letters. But *The Welsh Extremist* drew some 200 letters in the first six months. Of course this can't be much by the standard of best-sellers. It was the emotional character of so many of them that was both striking and worrying.

While it was agreeable enough to get an *englyn* from Dic Jones and the letters of friends, it was more unsettling to be told by my wife that a man wearing a bandolier had turned up at the back door to offer his services to the nation; but most worrying were the letters which said things like 'I went out into the fields and wept.' At this point one began to realize that writing a book is not just a matter of self-expression, but a social act, with possible social consequences.

A word about the publishing history. Gollancz, the original publishers, had no paperback imprint, so I approached a London paperback company where I had a contact. The initial editorial response was enthusiastic, but the book was eventually turned down because the company's Welsh sales manager said he could not put his heart into promoting such a book. This was rather typical of the pattern of response. In England, for which the book was intended, it was widely and favourably reviewed but disappeared without trace after a year; in Wales, for which it was not written, it produced very mixed reactions. Y Lolfa, who enterprisingly bought the paperback rights, initially found some shops refused to stock it, but over the years have sold the title steadily. The initial hostility was very much from a certain kind of Welsh speaker, whose servility was challenged, I suppose.

What I am trying to suggest is that the book is best seen as a moment in a social process which if fully described would include my own background and upbringing and those of all the people who reacted to the book; also the atmosphere of the time of publication, not in Wales alone. For what is striking in retrospect is that those years in Wales, in terms of rising expectation and style of protest, had much in common with what was happening in other places—Civil Rights in the north of Ireland and the USA, Paris, many of the other European minorites,

Québec. The book is thus social product and social trigger, and the pattern is particularly complicated because of language. The case put is the case for Welsh-speakers (perceived very largely as the case for Wales). That case was put to England, but it had the effect for Welsh-speakers (who had heard much better cases for their survival put in Welsh) of legitimizing their claims in the progressive English terminology of the times. My own background, Welsh-speaking by the skin of my teeth but brought up largely in England and beyond, though by no means unique, equipped me for this act of intercession and legitimization. Sensitive through language and family to the atmosphere of Welsh-speaking Wales, I had nevertheless avoided the acclimatization to prudence which a minority upbringing often implies. My kind of militant confidence was bound to alarm some, but communicated confidence to others, provided a vocabulary they could use. As for myself, the need to communicate between cultures, to join the two linguistic worlds of my experience, was a main motivating force, both in the writing of the book and in the founding of *Planet*.

So far I have placed commitment, values, what people might live for, or even die for, firmly within social processes. There are, of course, other possible grounds on which to base one's life: for example, religious values that claim to derive from a supernatural level. They are a matter of belief and cannot easily be argued with. Then there are secular 'humane' values which claim to transcend time and place—what were once called 'eternal verities'—but which, to my mind clearly always arise from and bear the marks of particular times and places. This good old liberal idealism is philosophically most unconvincing, even if most of us muddle along with some version of it a lot of the time. Then there is, or was, Marxism, with its insistence that human values are constantly made and remade by people in society. I go along with that statement if it stops there; in practice it never did and one was asked to go along with a lot else besides—historical inevitability, the class struggle, economism, base and superstructure, the reduction of ideas and literature and cultural effort to a kind of froth on the stream of economic forces. Raymond Williams found a way through this terminological jungle to what he called cultural materialism, a position that made a space within the social process for the creative efforts of individuals; he provided a conceptual frame within which, without distortion or amputation, I could fit my own experience.

It takes a foolhardy person to attempt to summarize any Raymond Williams position, but let me concentrate on one crucial Marxist term which he discusses and redefines: determination. Are our actions, our values 'determined' by wider social and economic forces? No, says Raymond Williams, not in the sense that we are pushed down the iron rails of inevitability by the locomotive of history; *that* he sees as a concealed idealist position, for an abstract force has been posited as transcending what people actually do, think, feel and create. But yes, of course, in another sense he finds that we are conditioned, and here he brings his characteristic etymological method brilliantly to bear on the question. The root sense of the word de-termine—the setting of boundaries (cf. Welsh *terfyn*/boundary and *pender-fynu*) brings out a different emphasis. When we are born, we enter into the life of a group that already exists; when we begin to speak, we enter into a language or languages; if we write, we enter into traditions of writing. In this sense the boundaries are set for us, we cannot avoid this degree of conditioning. And yet the pattern into which we enter is various and changing, the pressures on us are various and changing, each of us has a unique position within the more general pattern, and our reactions are consequently not wholly predictable. What is more, our effort within our inevitable limitations, our 'determination' in the everyday sense of 'resolve' to resist, to respond, to innovate or to reinforce existing pressures—all this in turn 'determines' (in the sense of 'conditions') the world into which a new generation enters. As Waldo Williams put it: 'Invention is the mother of what then becomes necessity.' Or David Jones: 'One is making a shape out of those things of which one is oneself made.'

This idea of being shaped and at the same time shaping can also be described as the transmission of values, not passive transmission of an accepted body of thinking, but active transmission of what has been inherited and tested and changed where necessary. The sense of generational transmission is extremely strong in Raymond Williams's novel *Border Country*, perhaps because the father passes on what he has known, more by what he is than by what he says; and throughout his critical work there is the resolve to rescue and transmit to the future the suppressed or ignored voices, those that have been excluded from selective accounts of literature or history. It is not surprising that reviewing *The Welsh Extremist* in *The Guardian* he should have welcomed it as a voice articulating an experience which English people did not know of, and should listen to. Nor, I think, was the idea of transmission absent from that moment of commitment when my children were playing in the field.

In the polemics that have surrounded Raymond Williams since his death, his admirers have rightly emphasized, in an atmosphere increasingly hostile to Marxist theory, his serious concern with the transmission of humane values. His enemies are keen to class him as outmoded, an ideological dodo in the bright consumerist world of today—that is one way of trying to cut off transmission. But I am not so sure that we are right to make a head-on contrast between what Raymond Williams represents and post-Modernism, defined for the moment as a condition where all meanings and readings and styles are co-existent and seemingly, therefore, equivalent. Things are more complicated than that. When everything has been said about the commercialization and technological proliferation which sometimes seem to make a great consumer supermarket of the arts and literature, it is still true that the sense of pluralism, of many voices and many readings of texts and of experience, derives in some measure from those very processes of liberation that occurred in the Sixties and Seventies and to which Raymond Williams contributed.

This perspective, which places transmission and continuity uneasily but perhaps also excitingly, within our consciousness of pluralism, can be brought to bear also on what has happened in the last twenty years in our country. First, a suppressed linguistic group became increasingly conscious of the pressures upon itself and exerted a counter-pressure. *The Welsh Extremist* and its author can be fitted into that dual pattern. The exertion of the counter-pressure was also a discovery of limits, the limits of a minority's strength. Some institutional gains were made by the Welsh language, and there were corresponding gains in respect and self-respect for Welsh-speakers. Language forms a kind of barrier that precariously defends what was then won. The national movement in English that had grown round the language movement in the Seventies soon fell away, having gained no institutions of its own. The revival of the south Wales radical tradition in the Eighties derived very specifically from the miners' strike of 1984-85 and briefly joined hands with the radicalism of Cymdeithas yr Iaith Gymraeg in the popular front atmosphere of the time, but is it likely to revive again with the almost total demolition of the coal industry? Will the writers of south Wales ever write again with the ebullient confidence that grew from that distinctive popular cultural base? At the end of Raymond Williams's *The Fight for Manod*, Mathew Price looks north to the old rural culture, and south to the valleys, and concludes 'they were both old now'. It seems to follow that we must imagine something new, which is rather what Gwyn A. Williams suggests when he sees Wales as a concept reinvented by the Welsh in every generation. But who are the Welsh? Some element of continuity must be implied in that term if it is to be a collective self-reconstruction.

So we are left, none of us where we thought we'd be, whether as Welsh-speakers or English-speakers, socialists, feminists or ecologists. Some gains have been made, yet the losses continue of most of the things that have been characterized as Welsh. However, we shouldn't perhaps expect that every period be one of total mobilization. Perhaps we perceive the national life in too dramatic terms. There is such a thing as political fatigue, as all will know who have thrown themselves into campaigns; and there is such a thing as keeping things going. Witnessing the cohesion of the peoples of Eastern Europe and beyond in their moment of national self-assertion, I am struck by the thought that these mobilizations were only possible because over many decades in most unfavourable conditions, those cultures had been kept going. In the relatively benign conditions of Wales we have made a perhaps less than adequate cultural effort. To make that effort might in the long run be the most political thing we could undertake, every bit as important as the more dramatic moments of self-revelation and self-definition represented by *The Welsh Extremist*.